Small Miracles

Prof. (Hon.) Architect ASKIN OZCAN

Outskirts Press, Inc.
Denver, Colorado

Dedication

With endless thanks to my parents Halil Er Ozcan and Muzeyyen Ozcan, to my relatives, friends and teachers; and with special thanks to Paul for his typing and corrections.

Contents

Introduction

Some people do not believe in God. To them I would like to say the following: countless species of life forms, each a unique organism, functioning in perfect balance and harmony from its inception to its birth, growth and death, cannot be accidental. There is a great wisdom and power, an almighty God, who has shaped all life and the universe. If there had not been an almighty God, and if all life and the universe had shaped itself, there would never be this perfect balance and harmony. We human beings understand so very little of the universe and its life forms, because we have not created them. We do not know the reason of the existence of life and of the universe. But with our sciences and arts, we study and learn their greatness and their rules.

Nature is the work of God. With all its material and metaphysical aspects, nature has its structure and function, although we understand so very little of it. We are part of this unexplainable mysterium and have a certain awareness of it, of its great complexity beyond our capabilities.

God has sent prophets to mankind so that they can explain to human beings that there is God. Their operation has always been surrounded with miracles so that human beings understand the existence of God. Prophets carried to mankind God's messages and order. Sciences and arts are not against religions, which are the order of God, but they are also the order of God to human beings. "No one will come to me in darkness," says the Bible. The Koran says: "Those who under-stand science, understand this book better." It also says "The place for those who create beauty, is the para-dise…." and "There is paradise and hell, both in this life and in the life to come!"

We are also made aware of God, through the small miracles God makes for us. There are so many exam-ples of them in our lives. Our mere coming into exis-tence is a miracle in itself. As we pray to God almighty, sometimes our prayers are accepted and we experience small miracles that solve our problems and help us. God sometimes talks to us as well, in a special way and answers our questions, warns us, helps us. Famous psychiatrist Thomas Szasz says, "when people tell us they are talking to God, we consider this normal, but when people tell us that God talks to them, we con-sider this abnormal. If it is normal for us to talk to God, it should also be normal that God talks to us."

Small Miracles is a collection of incidents that hap-pened to me personally. Some of them are clearly the acts of God. Others are disputable; they could be coin-cidences. I included all of them, so that the reader can decide for himself/herself.

The Koran: "Pray to God to make small miracles for you. This way, your believing in God becomes eas-ier."

Chapter 1
Two Spectacles in the Sky for "The Believers"

Many years ago, a good friend, Prof. Dr. Salvatore Caiozzo, who is now the chief priest of the Swedish orthodox church, gave me an interesting idea. "Why don't we unite all the religions of God?" he asked. Oddly enough, we happened to meet with him very often, totally unplanned, at odd times, odd places – some twenty or thirty times. Finally I asked him, "Professor Salvatore, what does God want from us so that he makes us meet so often at totally odd times and odd places?" He laughed. "Indeed," he said, "we are meeting very often with you totally unplanned, at very odd times and places!" These meetings turned into short but useful conversations about God and religions. I had no religious education at that time. I believed in God as a result of tradition and occasionally prayed to God. But I had never taken part in any ritual, either in a mosque (though "Moslem" is written in my Turkish identity papers), or in a church or synagogue. I had even thought that although there is God, he might have arranged sending his Books somehow from other civilizations in the universe. Turkey is a secular country and religious education of the children and the youth is not obligatory in the state schools, so nobody gets any religious education in the state schools. Those who attend religious courses outside the state schools are usually obliged to read the Koran in Arabic without understanding it.... So, in Turkey, religious education is quite weak for the average person. Of course, if one wants to study Islam or any other of God's religions, one has the possibility to study in the special schools and in the university. But the religious education is not incorporated into the general education. In the summer of 1960, just before I went to Germany for technical practice (at that time I was studying Architecture at the Middle East Technical University in Ankara), I had fifty Turkish Lira in my pocket and I saw the Koran in Turkish translation in the shop window of a bookstore. Its price was fifty TL. I pondered for a while whether I should buy it or have a nice kebab lunch in the adjacent restaurant. I decided to have a lunch, as I was quite hungry and I would not have time to read the Koran in Germany anyway. I could buy it upon my return after three months, I thought. Three months later, all of the copies of this Koran in Turkish were sold out and I could not buy it. I remembered hearing a voice, just before going to the kebab restaurant, "Buy the Koran now! Otherwise you'll regret!" I really regretted that I had not bought it. My contact with the Koran started in the year 2000.

I was in Istanbul during the summer of 2000 (at that time I lived in Stockholm, Sweden) and I was looking for the books of Yunus Emre, well-known Turkish folk philosopher. Suddenly I noticed on the shelves the Turkish version of the Koran. I bought it and read it many times. I also read the Bible after that, as the Koran says, "It came to confirm the other books God sent before it," and that "One shouldn't distinguish the God's prophets and books from one another."

I noticed that nearly all that was preached in the Koran and the Bible were the same. I noticed only a few differences that were not of the nature to cause any wars or conflicts among the religions of God. The books had come a long time ago and especially in the New Testament and the Old Testament and the Psalms (which came to the prophet David) a few shortages and changes were of the expected nature in the long time elapsed. The Koran, although unchanged in its original Arabic version, also manifested a few changes in its translations (the closest possible translations) into many languages.

Although all of these books came from God, and all the believers in God should be brethren, they have fought against one another throughout history. Not only that, but they also were divided within themselves and fought and had conflicts within themselves. Books, the Koran, the New Testament, the Old Testament, the Psalms, the Book of Mormon, and even the great books of Buddhism which believes in Nirvana (by which, God is meant), say the same things: peace, love, brotherhood, co-operations, respect for the self, for others, for the environment, for the parents; for truth and knowledge and beauty and justice; praying to God for mercy and benevolence and help, in small miracles; belief in the other world after death (life after death), respecting and obeying the God's prophets and books; the last day of judgement, self control and modesty, are mentioned in all the God's books. I did not notice a difference in the God's books to mankind, except a few, that are so

3

natural, thinking of the enormous time spans and cultural differences in the societies when these books came. These books are the volumes of the same "encyclopedia" God graciously sent as a blessing to mankind. They all glorify mankind and also the knowledge and beauty. Why these fights among the religions of God or within them? Why this fight between the scientists and the religions? Why this fight between the arts and the religions? Who is to blame? The misunderstandings lie on the part of the human beings – not elsewhere. Differences, fights, are in the minds – not in the books!

Thinking along these lines, I remembered Father Salvatore's suggestion: Why don't we unite all the religions of God? And I decided to start a movement called "The Believers". I sent out its newsletter to hundreds of friends. It contained paragraphs from the Bible and the Koran that were the same and showed the common grounds of the God's religions. It showed the necessity for believers in God to read all the books God sent to mankind and not just one of them. In this way, all prejudices and misunderstandings about the other religions would easily be erased and the friendship and brotherhood among various believers, in different religious groups would be enhanced. Many of my friends asked me the question: "Why do I have to leave my religion and join The Believers movement?" The answer is simple: No one should leave his or her religion to join The Believers, but bring his or her religion into The Believers and enrich this movement!

The Believers also stresses the unity between the religions and the sciences and the arts. Its newsletters clarify with reference to the Bible, to the Koran, to the prophets, and to the famous scientists and artists, that all human knowledge should be unified and integrated to be useful in the best way.

There are other groups around the world working on the same theme. And this is not a new movement. The Koran mentions: "Talk to the Christians and Jews. Tell to them your God is also our God, as God is one. Propose to them to build an Abraham's Nation together. If they accept, they will certainly be doing the most correct and the most beautiful."

The Bible has already said in the Old Testament, "Mankind will find peace in the Nation of Abraham."

Many Christians do not regard the Koran as a book of God, although it is very clear in the Koran that it came from God, and in the miraculous way it was dictated by God to Prophet Mohammed. In fact, it was a Christian priest who first recognized Mohammed when he was a Child, that he would be the next prophet. And it is said in Barnaba's version of the New Testament in the Louvre Museum, that Jesus has said to the people that the next Saviour would be Ahmed (Mohammed).

The Koran states clearly that it came to confirm the books God had sent earlier, the New and Old Testaments and the Zabur (the Psalms which came to the prophet David) and that "One should not distinguish one prophet from another and to those who hold all the God's prophets equally there is a big gift." And "one should not distinguish between the God's books" (Sora: Ali Imran, paragraph: 84).

One night in July 2001, as I was writing the newsletter of The Believers, I went to the balcony and prayed to God. I asked for a small spectacle in the sky to show me if I were on the right way with the work I was doing with The Believers movement. About half a minute later, a meteor fell, presumably at a very near distance, and spread up like an umbrella in many colors. This spectacle lasted for about forty-five seconds. I became breathless. I had asked God to make a spectacle for me, if I were on the right way, and there was a spectacle! I started to wonder whether it was really God who made it. This spectacle happened half a minute after my prayer. If it was not God who made it, then what a coincidence it was!

The following month, again, while writing the newsletter of The Believers, I went again to the balcony and said to God, "If it was you who made the spectacle last month, please make one more now, so I will know for sure it was you!"

Then I remembered the Koran and the Bible: "God is never to be tested!" and I apologized to God in front of all the stars and withdrew back my words. Right at that moment, a faint light came under the half moon and started to grow and grow and grow. I became afraid without having a chance to think about what was going on and went back into the living room and closed the door of the balcony. I then thought that it must have been a passing satellite that reflected the sun's rays. Then the grown light (it had become as big as a quarter moon) became smaller and smaller and finally became a faint spot again and continued leftwards. This spectacle, too, lasted for about forty-five seconds or a minute at most. I think both of these spectacles came from God. If they were only coincidences, then my praying to God came from God, at such times, when these two spectacles occurred in July and August – because two spectacles occurring one month apart, only half a minute after I prayed to God for a spectacle, cannot be coincidences!

God is with us every second. We are watched and

listened to and protected – or warned – or even punished by God, continuously. The more we listen to the books of God, the better it is for us, I think. To listen to the books of God we do not have to leave our sciences or arts. On the contrary, we must stick to them. Religions are not against the sciences and the arts; religions inspire, encourage and confirm the sciences and the arts. If human beings misunderstand this, it is the fault of the human beings.

If you would like to start a "Believers" movement in your region, you can. After reading our manifesto at the end of this book, you may continue further in your region. You must have first studied the Bible and the Koran, of course, and preferably all other books that came from God, like the Book of Mormon and the books of Buddhism, if you believe their leaders were also prophets.

The Believers movement will bring closer the believers in many of God's religions. In this way, Moslems will learn about Christians and Jews and Mormons and Buddhists, and they will learn about Moslems and about each other. As they learn about one another, they will learn more about God. The Believers movement can grow more meaningfully as scientists and artists are welcomed into it as well, as The Believers do not only aspire to unite all the believers of God, it also aspires to unite all the God's religions with the sciences and the arts.

Chapter 2
The Voice in the Sky

Year: 1963. I was visiting Ankara and my friends there, during the New Year's vacation while I was doing military service in southeastern Turkey as a teacher.

The night before I visited a good friend, Cemil, who worked as an economist at the TPAO (Turkish Petroleum Corp.) the following happened. While lying in the bed in the hotel room, I heard a voice inside me say that the next day an extraordinary accident would happen on the way to my friend. I asked God what exactly would happen. I got an answer:

I would swear at something and a stone under my foot would cause me to fall and hurt myself on the street. I started to wonder if I had become crazy. I did not pay too much attention to that. The next day I got off the "dolmush" (the shared taxi, which is a popular means of transport in Turkey) in front of the Swedish Embassy. My friend lived about one hundred meters from there. When I saw the Swedish Embassy, I swore at Sweden, because a Swedish girl -friend I had once (whom I was planning to marry) had left me to take a vacation in Paris alone, although I had moved from Turkey to Scandinavia for her sake. And once, my application for a scholarship to study in Sweden was rejected when I was getting many scholarship offers from other countries....laughable youngish reactions!

As soon as I swore, a frightening, loud voice shouted at me from the sky above the Swedish Embassy: "What do you want from these people? They will guarantee your future!" it said. I became so scared, I stepped on a small stone and lost my balance and fell on the ground. My new costume, which had cost me three month's salary was ruined and I started to bleed all over. I went immediately to my friend who was astonished, with good reason.

"What happened to you Askin?" he asked, "C'mon in." He helped me by first cleaning up my wounds and putting on some 'teinture d'iode,' a common disinfectant. My body, in the front, became brown all over. I told him the story. He was even more shocked after hearing it.

I asked a few psychiatrists afterward, if I were crazy. They all said such incidents occur, though scarcely, and they do not know how to explain them.

As I read the Koran the first time in the fall of 2000, a paragraph said, "Do not swear. If you do, you may hear the God's frightening, trembling voice, as God becomes angry and you would be very scared!" When I read these lines, I entered a shock. The Koran was telling the truth. I had already heard God's angry, trembling voice in December, 1963. The Bible also says, "Do not swear!" Is it possible not to believe in God after such truths?

Chapter 3
A Nice Coincidence

Before I was enrolled in the army as a teacher-officer, I had gone first for a military medical checkup at the local army office. After the checkup, I had entered the room where five officers (Military, Navy, Air Force, Gendarmary and Coast Guard) select the soldiers into their sections. The navy officer, Yildirim Findik, saw me and shouted, "Askin! What are you doing here?" He came near and told me that this selection room was for soldiers and as I had studied at the university for three years, I had the right to be a teacher-officer if I wanted. Yildirim Findik was a good friend of mine. I was surprised to see him as a navy officer. He explained that he finished the university and became a reserve navy officer, I had left the university and went traveling and working in Denmark in an architectural office with the reference of Prof. Architect Johan Otto von Spreckelsen, who was my teacher at the Middle East Technical University in Ankara, and who later won the first prize in the architectural contest for La Defense in Paris. I thought, not having finished the university, I would be enlisted as a soldier.

"No," said my friend Yildirim, "you can be a teacher-officer and would be sent to a village if you want."

"Ok," I said, "I didn't know that."

He gave me another address and gave me my papers and sent me to that other office. I was very lucky, as being a soldier in the Turkish Armed Forces can be a very tough task.

Soon after an interview at the other office, I was put on a train to Batman, then by bus to Siirt where we had a one-month orientation course before we drew our lotteries and sent to our respective villages.

If I had not met my friend Yildirim Findik in the selection committee, I would not know of the possibility that I could be a teacher-officer and would have instead been sent as a soldier, which is indeed a very tough and difficult job.

Chapter 4
Another Lucky Coincidence?

Or did God help me?

During my military service as a teacher, I was positioned in a village of Kozluk, named Yediboluk (Mushritan) – which was the only village accessible by a road. All the remaining teacher-officers were sent to remote villages accessible only by horse or mule. I was lucky in the lottery and drew that village, the only village on a road (thank God). It was some kind of a miracle too...

Yediböluk (Mushritan) was quite a primitive village, remote from civilization, remote from Istanbul where my family lived, or from Ankara where I had friends.

As I passed through Ankara in my New Year's holiday, in 1963, I stopped for a few days to visit my friends. As I was going to the campus of the Middle East Technical University to meet my friends, I was passing in front of the Ministry of Education. I noticed an announcement on a small blackboard placed in front of the Ministry, which read, "Today is the Minister's open house day, to meet with the public." It was a Saturday. The time was five to one p.m. Five minutes before the closing time of The Ministry...

As I read the announcement, the employee of the ministry who was standing at the door came and talked to me.

"Do you wish to talk with the Minister?"

"No, no!" I replied.

"Don't feel shy," he said. "He has five minutes more. He is talking with someone now who should leave soon. You have certainly time to meet him for a few minutes."

"No, no," I protested. "I don't want to meet the Minister."

"Oh, c'mon," he welcomed in a friendly manner. "Don't be shy! Are you a teacher?"

"Yes," I said, "I am doing my military service as a teacher-officer."

"The Minister will be very pleased to meet you, I am sure," he added and he took me into the Minister's office as the other man left.

Well, I was in the office of the Minister of Education. I had to say or ask something; otherwise it would look stupid coming into a minister's office without any reason.

"Welcome!" said the Minister, showing me to one of the comfortable armchairs in front of his huge desk. "What can I do for you?"

"I am doing my military service as a teacher-officer in a village in southeastern Turkey," I started.

"I see," he said. "How is the situation down there?"

I told him about the situation in a few minutes and added that I was too far away from Istanbul, where my family was, and too far away from Ankara, where my friends lived and how nice it would be if I could work in Istanbul or Ankara, although serving the country is equally honorable wherever the duty is....

"Do you speak any foreign languages?" he asked.

"Yes," I replied, "fluent English, average German."

"Well," he said, "maybe we could use an interpreter here in the Ministry.

"Really?" I glowed with happiness.

"Let me check with the Ministry of Defense," he said. "If we can get their permission, we need a few interpreters here and maybe I can employ you here."

Meanwhile, he asked for my ID card. He called the Ministry of Defense, but the result was negative. The Ministry of Defense did not permit the employment of the teacher-officers in large cities when villages were without teachers.

"It is a pity," he said. "Otherwise we could use you here." Meanwhile, he examined my ID.

"What is your father's name?" he inquired.

"Halil Er Ozcan," I replied.

"Come again!" He was astonished. Are you Halil Er's son?"

"Yes," I said.

"Well your father and I are good friends from the teacher's college. Don't you remember me, when you visited me with your father when I was the Chairman of the National Parliament? You were five or six years old then. You had started mingling my books and your father had scolded you not to do that. Don't you remember?"

"Vaguely, sir," I replied. "I remember visiting a gentleman, with my father, in the National Parliament when I was a child, but I don't recall you."

"It was me," he said. "So you are Halil Er's son!"

He offered me a change of jobs from the village I was positioned at in southeastern Turkey to a village near Ayvalik, in western Turkey, a nice resort. I would still teach as a reserve army officer, but in a village five minutes from Ayvalik, a beautiful resort in western Turkey, near Izmir, Pergamon, Troy. My father was very astonished at this coincidence. Soon I moved from Yediboluk to Gomec, near Ayvalik.

I found a three star hotel in Ayvalik, where my monthly salary would suffice for only two night's stay. But its owner was such a friendly man that he offered me a small room for one third of my salary for an entire month at his hotel, because I was doing my military service.

I checked into this hotel and had a marvelous time. As German tourist groups started to come in, in the Spring, I used to help them in the restaurant translating from German to Turkish and vice versa. The owner of the Hotel noticed this and made all the food free of charge for me for the rest of my stay there!

Once, a Turkish film company was filming in the town and I had the chance to
be friends for a month, with a famous film star (Belgin Doruk) playing in the film. I also met there a gentleman Teoman Madra who frequented the hotel and was one of the owners of a local olive oil and soap factory, With Teoman we became good friends. He was a jazz enthusiast and a photographer besides being an agricultural engineer.

Spending my time in the military in such a nice resort town like Ayvalik and working in
a near-by village as a teacher can not be classified as anything else, but a true miracle. I thank God, for being so kind and benevolent to me.

P.S. The name of the Minister of Education I met was Mr Semi Ergin. Actually, as I learned later, he was the Minister of Defense at that time, but worked as a substitute Minister of Education just for one day- that day when I happened to visit The Ministry of Education!!!

Chapter 5
I Flew in the Air

T he school inspector was going to come to the village to verify the work of the teachers. This was a very serious thing, both for the regular teachers, who would not get a salary increase if the inspector did not give them a positive report, and for the teacher-officers like me. An Inspector's negative report could cancel all of my military service completed so far and I would need to start my military service again, perhaps as a soldier.

I was usually on time to my work. But, that day when the inspector had come, I nearly missed the school bell. Teachers had to be in their classrooms before the school bell rang and they had to start the lesson when the bell started to ring.

When I entered the school garden, I noticed the inspector was waiting in front of my classroom! It was only a few seconds until the school bell would ring. I had to be in the classroom before the school bell rang. This was a very serious thing in Turkey.

I prayed to God to make me fly. And I flew about 3

meters, five-ten centimeters above the ground... I could not believe it. When I reached the classroom, the school bell started to ring.

"You are lucky," the inspector grinned. "As you know, teachers have to start their lessons when it rings."

"Yes," I said, hurrying into my classroom, "I don't have time to apologize."

I started my lesson on "traffic" to the fifth year students. At the end of the lesson, the inspector criticized my teaching.

"You should come at least a few minutes earlier to your lessons," he said. "And you don't need to teach so much theory. It would have been better if you took the students to the road and taught them the traffic rules there and how to cross the roads, etc."

"Yes, sir," I said, "you are right."

"But," he said, "I liked your way of joking with the students; they seemed to like you."

"Thank you, sir," I replied.

"I noticed you nearly flew in the air as you came. What happened?"

"I don't know sir; something happened," I said. I was shocked to have flown about 3 meters, about five, ten centimeters above the ground!

"Go talk with the principal," he said.

During the fifteen minutes recess, I discussed with the principal what happened. He was a very nice man. He explained to me that there is a religious sect in Turkey where members can make their weights disappear and fly in the air for some meters.

This was a very curious experience for me. It never happened to me again. I understand in India, some "gurus" can make the weight of things disappear with their mental powers. Such an experiment has been done at the UN, as I had read in a bulletin picturing a "Guru" together with the UN Secretary General, the then Soviet President and others beside a huge metal weight which the guru had lifted with one finger alone, having made its weight disappear by his mental power.

Chapter 6
My Father's Death

This is not only the saddest chapter in this book; it is also the saddest chapter in my life.

During the first summer vacation when I was working as a teacher-officer, we had the chance to be at home with our families. In the second summer vacation, we attended a basic military training. During the first summer vacation, I was happy to be at home in Istanbul. We also drove with my family to many places in western Turkey: Pergamon, Izmir, Cesme Beach, Kusadasi and Ephesus and my family met also teachers in my school where I worked. Both of my parents being teachers, they got along fine.

Upon return to Istanbul, my father started to indoctrinate me that after the army, I should either work or continue with my university studies. He said that if I continued studying, he would help me financially. If I started to work, I should help my family financially.

All of this sounded fine and logical to a mature person, but my interests were different as a young man. I wanted to travel after the army. I wanted to go back to

Denmark where I had worked before my army service. And visit Sweden and a few girls with whom I was exchanging letters. My father strongly opposed this. He said, "It is enough traveling you did. You have been one year in the USA as an AFS exchange student. One summer you went to Norway with a scholarship. The next summer you worked in Germany. You left your university studies and worked one year in Denmark! You can't just travel and travel like a rolling stone! You have to establish yourself somewhere! You will be 24 soon!" We had a definite conflict.

I prayed to God to help me. I said to God, "Dear God, solve this situation!"

My father died two and a half months later at the age of 51. He got a heart attack and that was his third one. He smoked heavily, was under stress after a traffic accident, drank coffee and was overweight. Of course, I have suffered since then, since 1963, when we lost him. My suffering is much more because it might have been my wish from God. I can't excuse myself.

****

My advice to people: "Be kind to your parents. Listen to their advice and not only to your own wishes. Because if you loose them, without having done as they wanted you to do, you suffer and may blame yourself later for not having listened to them enough!

You are in this world because of your parents. Be thankful to God and to your parents for that!

Chapter 7
Miracles in Scandinavia

A fter my military service, I worked briefly in Istanbul and then traveled to Germany, where I
worked for an American company briefly and then I
headed for Copenhagen. Prior to my military service, I
had worked for a year at an architectural office in Copenhagen and hoped I would find a job again in the
same field.

Much to my surprise, building credits had been cut
down and architectural offices did not need any personnel. I stayed with a Danish family as a guest whom I
had met in Ayvalik, Turkey. But soon my money was
finished and I had only one crown left in my pocket.

I decided to go to the Turkish Embassy the next day
and borrow money to return to Turkey. My Danish
host said that as it was my last day with them, he
wanted to invite me to the Tivoli Gardens that evening.
"The whole family would enjoy that," he said.

So we went to the Tivoli Gardens after dinner. I
noticed a lottery stand where the tickets cost one crown.
The biggest prize was a big Danish cheese, maybe

weighing fifty or sixty kilos.

I owed a lot to this Danish family. I wondered how I could repay them. A thought passed in my mind. If I bought a lottery ticket with my last crown and won that big cheese, how nice it would be to give it to them. I prayed to God to make me win that cheese and I bought a ticket.

Yes! I had won the cheese! The lottery salesman made a few minutes of advertising by shouting, "Attention! Attention! Here is a lucky winner! He won the biggest prize! A very big cheese!"

Then he gave me a coupon, which we had to take to the cheese factory to get the cheese. I was indescribably happy. I gave the coupon to my host, Hilmar, an engineer. "Here," I said, "I owe you so much. Perhaps this will partly pay for it!" They became happy too.

The next day, as I had no money, I had to walk to the Turkish Embassy. I sincerely hoped that they would lend me money to return to Turkey. Or else I would not know what to do. My host offered me a small monetary help, so I would not need to walk all the way to the embassy, but I refused. I decided to walk, even though it would take a few hours.

On the way, I think it was Hellerup, I noticed a sign on a building, "Employment Office". I went in. I explained my situation to a lady officer. She said she could not offer me a job, but she suggested I contact the Royal SAS Hotel, as they needed personnel. This was sometime in the autumn of 1965.

Instead of going to the Turkish Embassy, I went to the Royal SAS Hotel. I was hungry, thirsty and tired walking. I talked to the personnel manager. He said he needed a few people in the kitchen to wash glasses, dishes, help with simpler chores and he would be willing to employ me if I had a work permit. I had none.

I said, "Give me a few days. Let me talk to the Danish Police, maybe I can get a work permit."

"It takes months of waiting for a work permit," he said. "But if you want to try it, I give you time, till tomorrow 7 am. Go and talk to the Foreigners' Department at the Police. They are very near here, a few hundred meters, but they will close soon! If you come here with a work permit by tomorrow at 7 am, I'll give you a job. Otherwise, forget it!"

This was one of the biggest miracles in my life. I knew it would not work, I knew I could not arrange a work permit within a few hours, but I wanted to try.

I went to the Police's Foreigners' Department, very near the Royal SAS Hotel. There was a long queue of applicants from many countries. I approached the window where a woman officer with a broken arm was receiving applications. Everyone in the line was shouting at me, "Go to the back of the queue!" To the woman officer, I said in my broken Danish, which I remembered from two years ago, "What happened to your arm?" She looked at me and pointed to the door beside. "Come from here," she said. I went in.

"What do you want?" she asked.

I explained my situation, half in Danish, half in English, and said, "I have a job offer from the Royal SAS Hotel, but they need to see a work permit tomorrow by 7 am." I added, "I must work. I have no money left."

She understood the situation. She said, "Go to the SAS Hotel and tell them you talked with me, give them my name and telephone number and they can call me. You may work there until you get an official work-permit. And tomorrow, you can come here to fill your application form for a work-permit…processing your application can take some months."

I thanked her… I was flying in the air, because of happiness. I thanked God. I had experienced another miracle!

I walked to my friend's house – I don't know how many hours. I told him the story. I said, now you can lend me some money and I shall pay you from my first weekly salary. He lent.

On the table was a big wheel of Danish cheese.

"It was difficult to get this into the car," he joked. "I don't know how we shall fit it into the fridge! We have to cut it into many pieces.

The next day I enjoyed the luxury of a streetcar to the SAS Royal Hotel. I was at the personnel manager's office at 7 am sharp.

"What happened?" he inquired.

"I may work," I said. "You can call this police-woman, when they open at 9 o'clock. I handed to him her name and number. It will take some months for them to process my application and give me an official work permit, but I may work until then," I explained. The personnel manager was shocked like I was.

"It is unbelievable, but it is good!" he said. He gave me a job washing champagne glasses in a machine. I worked there for three months. All food was free of charge. I had found a room nearby. I saved much money. After three months, I went to visit a Swedish girl in Skagersvik, near Mariestad, in Sweden, with whom I had corresponded for two years. I had about 1000 Swedish crowns in my pocket.

In Sweden, I worked at small jobs for a few months. In that time, I sent job applications to airlines in Scandinavia, as I was interested in working for an airline. I received over twenty negative replies and one positive reply from British European Airways in Oslo, where the manager said that he just got transferred from Istanbul to Oslo, and he liked Turkey and Turks, and could give me a job at Oslo Fornebu Airport in the spring, if I spoke sufficient Norwegian by then, as he needed six new personnel there.

I visited Oslo and met Mr. Drury, the BEA's manager there. He suggested that I could also work in Istanbul, as they wanted to employ someone for the sales office. The weather was so cold, one of the coldest winters since many years they said. I saw minus 35 first time in my life. In the New Year's Eve walking from a restaurant to the Youth Hostel, I nearly froze. They kept me half an hour in zero degree, before permitting me come into the plus 20 degree hall of the youth hostel. They said this was necessary as, if I went directly from 35 minus to 20 plus, I can die!!!

The BEA manager suggested that, it would be better for me to return to Istanbul and work in the BEA there and that he would send them a reference about me. If it shouldn't work out, then I can return to Oslo, but I must learn some Norwegian meanwhile.

I bought some books to learn Norwegian and a train ticket to Istanbul through
many countries and enjoyed a long train journey. In Istanbul, after some waiting, I was employed by the BEA.

Chapter 8
New Miracles

W hile I worked at the BEA office in Istanbul, several miracles occurred there too.

1 – We had a frequent London traveler, a Turkish lawyer, Mr Necdet Cobanli, who had a hotel and a travel agency in London. One day he mentioned that he needed a new manager for his travel agency, as the existing manager was to go to his military service in Turkey. I told him I was interested. He arranged a work permit for me and after a year's service at the BEA in Istanbul, I became the manager of A.T.A. Tourism Ltd. in London. This was a true miracle for me to get a chance to work in London.

2 – Before I went to London, my aunt in Istanbul introduced me to an interesting man, an old chemist who had studied at the Weimar University before the war, and had many interesting patents. One of them was for the production of

nicotine-free cigarettes, from the green salad (lettuce). He could, with the treatment of essences and some other chemicals, produce nicotine-free cigarettes, whose taste matched with the known brands! He asked me to find the proper channels to produce these cigarettes. We even signed a contract. This connection turned into a real miracle, as you will read in the following chapters.

In London, I did not find time to deal with the Nicotine -free Cigarette project, as I was busy with the travel agency, with seeing London and with a French beauty, about whom you will read also in the coming chapter.

Chapter 9
London Miracles

I got adjusted easily to the job as the manager of A.T.A. Tourism Ltd. in London. I was staying at the owner's hotel and made a few acquaintances there, but I was experiencing loneliness. I was missing the lively social atmosphere with friends at the BEA in Istanbul and my close friends. I prayed to God to solve this situation so that I would find a good, close friend in London, which is easier said than done, if one is a stranger in London. Shortly thereafter, I met one of my best class friends from Ankara, Onur, in the entrance to the Piccadilly Circus tube station. He looked at me and I looked at him! He had a pipe, a hat and a trench coat, was dressed like a typical Englishman. After a few seconds of shock, we shouted at each other and embraced each other. Since that day, we have spent most of our free-time together. His wife, Tijen, also a classmate of ours, cooked delicious dinners and I used to take a good bottle of wine to them and the discussions and fun would last until the late hours.

The second miracle that happened to me in London

is equally interesting:

One day, a beautiful French girl came into the travel agency looking for a job as an au-pair. My friend Onur was looking for someone to take care of his two-year old son, so that his wife could work. I have told this French girl this and asked her to come Saturday around one o'clock, so that I could take her to my friend Onur's. She came on Saturday and we went together to my friend. But, unfortunately his wife got a little jealous and did not want her. And I lost contact with that French girl. I had given her my phone number, but she hadn´t given me hers… I had fallen in love with her! Days and weeks passed and she did not call, though she had promised. I became sad.

One day, as I usually do, I went down during my lunch break, to the Piccadilly Circus to buy a Times. It was sold out. A tall girl was standing there reading the Swedish paper Dagens Nyheter. It stood out in big letters: Earthquake in Turkey, with a half page photograph from the earthquake area… I asked her if she would be kind enough to translate briefly, what had happened in Turkey and explained that I was Turkish and the Times was sold out and I wondered about the earthquake.

"Yes, I know," she said. "I wanted to buy a Times as well. No more left today. Of course, I'd be pleased to translate to you what it says here about the earthquake."

We sat on a bench nearby, in a small park-like place, and she translated for me the news. I offered her a coffee and a whisky as my token of appreciation. She said she had no time, but I would be welcome to her hotel after my work. She gave me the address and we agreed to meet at six o'clock at her hotel.

30

I went to her hotel at six o'clock. It was a two storey high small hotel in Bayswater. I gave the receptionist the name of the Swedish girl, and as he was looking for her room number, in the book in front of him, I also eyed the book a little, and I saw also the name of the French girl who had disappeared. Dominique!

"Is she staying here too?" I questioned.

"Yes," replied the receptionist. "Do you know her too?"

"Yes," I said. "I am looking for her."

"Well," said the receptionist, "the Swedish girl you are looking for stays in room number 5 and the French girl you are looking for stays in room number 1, except the French girl just left the hotel now. I don't know when she comes. She hasn't paid for ten days now, between you and me."

After hearing that the French girl had just left, immediately before I came into the hotel, I decided to go out and look for her and forgot about the Swedish girl.

"Sir," said the receptionist, "if you meet the French girl, please remind her to pay for the hotel, OK?"

"Yes, yes," I said, "I will."

I looked around for the French girl, for one hour. No trace of her. About a week later, the French girl called me at my office, apologized for not calling for such a long time and explained that she did not go to work for my friends, as my friend's wife had become jealous of her, and she did not want to create a problem in my friend's family and she did not call me because I was not her type.

"Wait a minute!" I exclaimed. "Don't hang up! I have something to tell you!" And I explained that I was in love with her and looked for her all around London and found her hotel in Bayswater. And I demanded that she must meet me to have a drink, at least!

"It is interesting," she said.

The next week, we met and never left one another! Our adventure lasted for years. This is a special story, which could be a book and a film.

I mentioned only that part, the beginning, which was a clear miracle, for me. To find someone in London, with her twelve million population, the way I did, cannot be a coincidence.

After a year in London, the owner of the travel agency decided to sell it and the hotel and return to Turkey and continue with his old job as a lawyer. I had to return to Turkey as well, after his decision. Luckily, Travel Trade Gazette International of London was looking for foreign correspondents. I applied for the post in Turkey and they gave me the job.

I was going to work in Turkey as a foreign correspondent with a blue press card, given to foreign journalists. All in-city travel by bus and boats was going to be free of charge, as well as all football games and other sports events and train travel within entire Turkey too. Air travel within Turkey would cost half as much. Maybe this was also a small miracle, as I returned to Turkey!

Chapter 10
The Nicotine-Free Cigarettes

Year: 1968. Place: Istanbul, Turkey. An autumn morning, I woke up shaken and puzzled after a nightmare. A strange and strong voice was telling me that soon a very important thing would happen in my life. I was wakened by the same shaking voice a few more times in the same week. What could happen in my life? I was twenty-eight, working as a reporter for the Travel Trade Gazette international, in Turkey. Being officially a resident of the UK, I had to leave Turkey every four months, even if it may be for a few hours, to keep my resident status in the UK, as a requirement of the Turkish law. Otherwise, being a Turkish citizen at that time, I would face difficulties in getting a passport and a permit for foreign traveling, unlike now.

I was also helping the Turkish chemist-inventor who held patents for an interesting product, a nicotine-free cigarette. I was promoting his invention and corresponding with possible financiers, distributors, and cigarette manufacturers.

The coming weekend, I headed for Edirne, the border town in Turkey. I spent the Friday night at a hotel in Edirne, after visiting the famous mosque of Architect Sinan, the Selimiye Mosque, and the next morning I went outside the town to try to catch a good- hearted driver to carry me into Bulgaria. It was raining. There were only a few cars passing by in the dead season of tourism. I saw a queue of twelve trucks carrying cement to Bulgaria. I went to the first one and asked the driver if he could take me into Bulgaria, only a twenty minute ride from there. The driver said he was heading for the northern Bulgarian city of Dimitrovgrad and that there was nothing spectacular there. I insisted that he could drop me off right after the border and I could shop right there in the Bulgarian duty-free shop and return back to Turkey. I explained that I had to make an exit and entry, to have the stamps in my passport. He said the border police do not like them to take hitchhikers, and so he did not take me. I asked the same thing of the drivers of the eleven other trucks in the line. They all gave me the same answer: "No!" I nearly gave up and was not going to ask the last one. But, I thought, one never knows. It might happen that he would take me. He did. He told me unlike the others, he was going west and that there was a nice little village after half an hour ride in Bulgaria, named Haskovo, the dwellers of which were mostly Turkish. And that every Sunday, there was a festival up on the hills and the villagers or any visitor could go up there and enjoy it.

Soon, we were at the border. I got my stamps in my passport and half an hour later I was in Haskovo. I checked into the only hotel in town, which cost only a dollar, including breakfast. The next day, I went to the festival of the village, which was more like a picnic up on the hill, the public bus carrying everyone to there and back free of charge. Among fat villagers, I had a few beers, feta cheese and olives with fresh bread. Some villagers were dancing to the accordion music. I was bored after an hour and returned to the village. My plan was to rest awhile, then have a dinner at the hotel, then to wander around the village and talk to the people in the coffee shops, overnight in the same hotel at one dollar, including breakfast and return to Turkey, the next morning, the same way – hitchhiking. Haskovo wasn't so exciting, but still was interesting with its Turkish population, inexpensive luxurious hotel, which had only a few tourists at that time of the year and a very gorgeous restaurant with a seven-piece orchestra. A complete dinner wasn't more expensive than a night there either.

I rested in my room until seven pm and read also the few brochures I had found in the hotel. Then I went to the restaurant. Soon the waitress came, and we chatted a few minutes, being familiar with one another from the previous day. I ordered a Wiener schnitzel. The orchestra was playing really fine music.

Suddenly a tall man came to my table and asked if he could sit with me. First, I thought this was a little strange as there were at least twenty five other tables, all empty, but I said, "Of course, you are welcome to sit here." A while later a conversation started.

"What are you eating?" he asked.

I got a little angry, as this was not the question one should ask a complete stranger.

"I am having a Wiener schnitzel," I said, "but they have a lot of other dishes. You should ask the waitress for a menu. Maybe you would like to have something else!"

"That is right," he said and called the waitress. He started speaking to the waitress in Bulgarian and ordered some things.

"Where are you from?" I asked.

"The States."

"How come you speak Bulgarian? Are you of Bulgarian origin?"

"Oh," he said, "I am a professor of Slavic languages and history." I was interested. "And you?"

Right at that moment, my eye caught the sight of a small box in the small pocket of my jacket, which I had forgotten to leave at home, in Istanbul. It contained a few nicotine-free cigarette samples. I became both angry at myself for having forgotten to leave them at home, as it could cause me very long interrogations if the customs officer found them, but also happy for having taken them with me, by mistake.

"Well," I said, "I am a reporter for the Travel Trade Gazette International in Turkey and I also deal with a new industry."

"What is it?" he inquired.

"Nicotine-free cigarettes," I said. "I am helping an inventor to find a financier to produce these nicotine-free cigarettes." I handed the box to him.

He smelled the cigarettes, looked at them and asked, "Can I try one?"

"Sure," I said. He took a cigarette and said he would try it in his room later. The cigarettes were patented in eight countries. They were in different tastes, and contained no nicotine. They were made from lactuca sativa, the salad green, which has the closest structure to tobacco, yet containing no nicotine. The inventor perfumed them with the same fragrances as real cigarettes. After dinner, we went into my room, talked more and the professor tried the cigarettes.

"How much do you need to produce these?" he asked.

"I don't know," I replied. "I am trying to find a market for them first."

"Did you get any orders?"

"Yes," I said. "From Japan, from Germany, from Africa …there are a few orders."

"Would you like to do this business with me?"

"It is possible," I said. "We are waiting for an answer from a few cigarette manufacturers, from Finland, from Germany, from Africa…."

He told me that he had some capital and could help us manufacture the cigarettes in the United States as a small industry. I invited him to Istanbul to meet the inventor and to discuss with him the conditions and to see his laboratory and take with him more samples if he wanted.

The next day, we were on our way to Istanbul to meet the inventor, Mr. Hilmi Gumushan. The inventor had previously tried to produce and market the cigarettes with a local capital holder and was cheated. He was now trying to find his way to produce his invention with another group, preferably on a small scale. Many companies were responding positively to our enquiries and were showing willingness to buy these nicotine-free cigarettes, if we produced them. A few cigarette factories were holding tests and we were waiting for their final answers. After meeting and discussing with the inventor Mr. Gumushan, the professor C:B. was very interested in this project.

"OK," said the professor, "I will go back to the States, discuss this business with my friends and my lawyer and most probably, we can invite you to the States, in a month from now. I can finance your stay, the organization of this business, further research on the matter, if necessary, small scale production and marketing of these cigarettes."

In a month's time we received two PAN AM tickets to Boston, a notarized agreement and an invitation to the States. We obtained our visas for the US and headed to Boston. I still have my Turkish passport with the US visa and the entry stamp to the USA, at Logan Airport in Boston, dated November 11, 1968.

The customs officer quickly located our sample cigarettes with the help of his dog and let us go, after a brisk inspection. Everybody looked at the hand rolled cigarette samples, as the customs officer inspected them and the custom's dog sniffed them. After showing our lab reports, the customs officer was satisfied and closed down the investor's suitcase, and wished us a success with our project.

There we were! We were in Boston, with a stock of nicotine-free cigarette samples, patented, and we had found a financier to help produce these cigarettes. I often thought of the shaking nightmare and of the voice telling me a very important thing would soon happen in my life, in Istanbul.

We established soon a small lab for our investor, to carry on his research and produce the required samples. We were going down to New York often to buy chemicals – of which we needed only a few grams – and which were being sold in gallons. Often, chemical companies were giving us free of charge, the few grams of chemicals we needed. Sometimes we were overnighting at people's houses, whom we met on the train or bus, or at a New York donut shop. Once, we overnighted at a hotel in Manhattan and had a problem coming to it, as an incident had occurred and the police had blocked the entrance to the subway, and were sending people away from the subway. Boston, at the time, was still quite a safe town, especially Cambridge, where we lived, but New York was already frightening, with its street crime. I thought the USA was the best and most dangerous country to live in. I still think the same.

On one side, inventor Mr. Gumushan was trying to produce perfect cigarettes in his laboratory, with less tar and the right fragrance, on the other, we were trying to complete the legal agreements with the financier and to compile a prospectus for our new industry. I was responsible from the international sales development and was corresponding with many distributors outside the USA, sending them samples. After the completion of our financial prospectus, which contained technical and financial data to start our new industry, we started looking for the required capital of 1.8 million dollars. Our professor friend who stood for the initial financing, had provided 100,000 dollars, which was to be spent for the lab, for our upkeeping, until the bigger financing was found, for the market research and for the search for machinery and a production possibility.

We soon learned cigarette manufacturing machinery could only be bought by the members of the large cigarette manufacturers' trust, which monopolized the entire market. But we met a man in New York who had previously worked with alternative methods of manufacturing nicotine-free cigarettes. He advised us that small manufacturing machinery could be bought on the black market and the cigarette manufacturers' trust would not mind if a company manufactured on a small scale. He told us where we could obtain such machinery. This encouraged us in our seeking the required capital of 1.8 million dollars. About half would be sufficient to purchase the machinery and the operational capital and the other half would be used for advertising. We knew that breaking into the market where people were addicted to nicotine containing cigarettes would be very difficult, but we thought if people bought one package for the purpose of trying, we would make a lot of money still. Then, not all people were addicted to nicotine. Some new starters who had not still developed addiction to nicotine, could also be won by our nicotine-free cigarettes.

My suggestion to the group was to start small, in someone's garage and try the market with a few thousand cartons of our nicotine-free cigarettes per day. Then we would slowly enlarge the business. My partners, mostly Harvard men, said that everything in the USA is done on a big scale, and they wanted to go public right away, and also profit from the price hike of the shares, parallel to the profit to be made from the sales.

Finding financing was difficult. One February evening, we had a discussion at the 34th floor of a New York bank where the assistant general manager told us that in the USA every four years venture capital could easily be found for such new and adventurous projects. He said it was difficult then, right in the middle of a slump to find capital for such projects. "If you came two years ago or if you come two years from now, I could find not 1.8 million dollars, but 18 million dollars for your project." He then offered us anyway, a financial package, whereby the bank would give us 12.5% of the shares of our industry and keep for itself and the presumable financier they would have the other 87.5% of the shares. This was unacceptable to us and we thanked the bank's assistant general manager and walked away. Had he offered us 20%-25% of the shares we would have accepted.

Later we contacted Bravo Industries, which were already producing nicotine-free cigarettes in Texas, based on a different patent. Their inventor and ours met once in a New York hotel and exchanged ideas and had a friendly talk, being of the same kind. Their inventor-chemist was an Armenian who spoke some Turkish. Our inventor, Mr. Gumushan was a Turk, who studied at the old Weimar University in Germany before World War II. He later held jobs as a pilot in the Turkish Army, as chemist in Istanbul and Libya and also as a bomb expert for the weapon factory of the new Turkish Republic. He had written many books and had many patents from many countries on diverse subjects. He was 67 years old at that time and was tremendously enjoying starting a new industry in the USA. Finally, we could not find the necessary 1.8 million dollars to start our nicotine-free cigarette industry. Had my American partners accepted to enter manufacturing on a small scale, as I had advised, probably we would have today a flourishing nicotine-free cigarette industry, selling well, but within the margin, not to anger the big boys of the market.

After six months´ trial, we all separated from each other. The inventor returned to Turkey, I went to Canada as an immigrant and our professor friend continued with his job. Sometimes as I clean the dust on the old books and files, I take in my hand our prospectus we had prepared then, turn its pages, recall my pleasant memories of our trial to start a new industry in the USA, and above all, my nightmare when I heard a voice that, "soon an important thing would happen in my life," when I was in Istanbul, before my trip to Bulgaria.

A box of sample nicotine-free cigarettes, I threw into the St. Lawrence River in Montreal, as I lost hope of realizing this project and watched this dream sail away.

I heard, after sometime, the inventor-chemist Mr Gumushan had returned to the USA, and later traveled to the Netherlands in pursuit of this project. I don´t know if he succeeded as I have not heard from him again .We had a binding notarized agreement between us, stating that I should get a certain percentage from the proceeds of any profit this business should bring. I received no news, no money.

Chapter II
The Parcel

Year: One thousand nine hundred and sixty nine. I was staying with the Turkish inventor-chemist in a South Boston apartment. As I have related in the former chapter, Chemist Hilmi Gumushan had patented his invention, the Nicotine-free cigarette, in eight countries and was in the USA with me, to produce them. Our partner Professor C.B.,was a Harvard-educated man interested to make big money in a short time, like many Americans do. Everyone had heard of us in Cambridge, Mass., where our company, Cambridge Tobacco Research Co., was located. People pointed out to me in the pubs, as the future millionaire. I had a large circle of friends there, perhaps for this cause.

I had a Finnish fiancée at that time, Anne. She was working as au-pair in the home of a psychiatrist. We were planning to get married. She wanted to study sociology, but first she wanted to make some money.

She was giving a birthday party sometime in February, I believe. I was of course invited as the chief guest. The birthday party was at two o'clock.

I went down from my apartment around half past twelve. I wanted to cash a cheque as usual, at the grocer below, buying a small chocolate or some chewing gum, as I knew the grocer and then buy a scarf in a shop across the street. But I found out the grocer was sick that day. His son who looked after the shop, did not know me and refused to cash my cheque.

As the grocer's son did not help me, I crossed the street and asked the shop there if they would accept a cheque if I bought a scarf. The answer was "no". I was stuck. There was no other shop around to buy anything, and even if there were, I had no cash and shops did not accept cheques, unless one knew the owner.

I couldn't go to my fiancée's birthday party without a present! I thought of not going to the party, but Anne was waiting for me and probably told her friends that I was coming. It would be a big disappointment for her.

I was thinking on the sidewalk about what I should do. Time was running out! Suddenly a big truck stopped in front of me at the red light. Then it took off at the green with such speed that its back doors opened and a parcel flew out to the road. I wanted to take the parcel, but I was afraid that someone might see. But, there were only two persons around, one on a side street about a hundred yards away, the other on the main road about two hundred yards away. I went to the middle of the road and picked up the parcel. My first thought was to put it into the mailbox on the corner, but as I inspected the parcel, I noticed the address was ripped off. It could neither go to the addressee nor to the sender!

I took it to the apartment and opened it. There was a knitted yellow blouse and a dark blue skirt in it! I wondered if it would suit Anne! I removed the price tag, which read eighty-six dollars and ninety cents, at that time a secretary's weekly salary. I took off the label on the box as well as I could and put the dress into the box and wrapped it with a nice paper.

Well, I was on the road again waiting for the bus. I had no idea whether the present would fit Anne, but at least I had a present with me! After reaching her home after an hour and after the customary rituals of kissing and hugging, I gave her the present. She opened it and blushed and got angry.

"Why on earth are you buying such an expensive present for me?"

"Well, it is your birthday and I thought you might like that!" I answered.

"If you had to do that, you should have asked me and we could go together and buy something that would suit my measurements!" she grumbled.

"Ah, if it doesn't fit you, we can always change it or I will buy you another one." I played rich.

"Actually," she said, "These are my favorite colors!" Then she put the clothes on and saw that not an inch had to be changed.

"How did you know my measurements?" she asked.

"Well, you are my fiancée, aren't you?" I joked.

She was very happy to get such a nice present. But she did look for a few seconds at the somewhat scratched box.

"The stupid salesgirl," I blamed, "I told her to make a nice package!"

"Oh, it doesn't matter!" she said, with a slight suspicion in her mind, which I could see from her eyes. She kissed me and thanked me. And I thanked God! This was one of the biggest miracles in my life.

Chapter 12
More Small Miracles in Cambridge, Mass.

During Christmas Eve of 1968, I had a funny feeling. I lived then, as said, with the Turkish chemist-inventor in a South Boston apartment. Mr. Gumushan, the chemist was watching the TV and I was lying in the bed around four pm. Something was urging me to go to the Idler, a popular pub in Cambridge. I was there the day before and they had put a notice on the door that it would be closed on Christmas Eve. In spite of that, why was I getting this urge in me to go there? The urge was so strong, that I got up, dressed and went. There was no one on the streets. It was an half an hour walk. There was some snow on the streets. I passed though the garden of Harvard University, then to the Harvard Square and a block further was The Idler. It had the same notice on its door. They were" CLOSED" for the day. "Stupid me," I thought. "If you follow all these crazy urges in you, you'll get to many places like this for nothing!" I turned back. Whom do I see, but Anne, my Finnish girlfriend with whom we had broken off sometime ago. There she stood in front of me.

"Come, let's make up and be friends again. It is Christmas today," she said.

"Ok," I said. Then I had understood the urge, which pushed me to come to the Idler, even though I knew it was closed. It was not a stupid urge.

"Do you have anything to do now?" she asked.

"No," I answered. "Something urged me to come here, although I knew the Idler was closed." I sounded astonished.

"Same with me," she said. "I knew it would be closed, but I came to check anyway. If you have nothing to do now, I invite you to a party. Do you want to come?"

Instead of going home and being with the old chemist, I was attracted to go to a party with Anne.

"Ok," I said. "I will come." She became glad. We walked together to the house of a professor of architecture, where Anne's girl friend, another Finnish girl worked as an au-pair. The professor was the chairman of the architectural school at Harvard. He and his wife, a famous painter, had just come from Scotland and had no friends yet in Cambridge. They were spending a lonely Christmas like us, with two Finnish au-pairs and a young Turkish man, who had studied architecture for three years, and had left his studies, and now was doing business in Cambridge.

We had a very interesting evening and discussion. I admired the paintings the professor's lady had painted, understandably one of the most famous painters in Scotland.

Chapter 13
Going Back to Architecture

After six months of hard work, our nicotine-free cigarette business in Cambridge had failed. I had already made an application for an immigrant visa to Canada, and during the last days of my stay in Cambridge, I received my visa.

I went to Canada. First, I was sent to a French language course in Quebec City. Later, I worked for half a year at Grace Kennedy Import-Export firm as a trader in Montreal. Then I became unemployed. I was receiving nearly as good a salary while unemployed, as in my work. I had to find a good job or continue with my education. I moved to Toronto, where employment possibilities seemed better.

One day, walking on College Street, I came across a dusty construction site. I passed to the other side of the street. Right in front of me was the University of Toronto, School of Architecture. There stood a sign, "Today is the last day of the students' exhibition of their work." Having studied architecture for three years before, in Ankara, I got interested. Just as I was going into the school, a professor was coming out.

"Are you coming to see the exhibition?" he asked.

"Yes," I said, "is it open?"

"Well, I was just leaving and wanted to close, as no one is coming to the exhibition, but if you want to see it, I won't close!"

"No, no!" I said. "Please go ahead and close it."

"No," said the gentleman at the door. "If you wish to see the exhibition, you are welcome." And he took me in, introduced himself as Professor Barker, gave me a cup of coffee and we toured the exhibition together.

"You seem to be interested in architecture," he commented. "Why not study further here?"

After a few days, I went to see him again with all my papers and student projects.

"Hmm," he said. "Your student projects are interesting. Your theory marks are quite high, but you have failed in a number of courses. The best thing for you is to take some courses in connection with architecture, get good marks and come back next year."

I did so. First, I applied for a paid course, in marketing, for the unemployed, by Canada Manpower. Then I got into York University's evening studies in urbanization. I was studying day and night.

The next year I got a part time job at Wellesley Hospital, working as a records clerk in the evenings and weekends and I also applied to the University of Toronto School of Architecture to enter with advanced standing into the third year. With some hurdles, I managed. It was hard to both study and work, but with the help of God, I managed. If all these aren't miracles, here is a miracle that happened in the last year of my studies.

I had a good class friend, Antti. He was a member

of the Communist Party. I had saved a thousand dollars and that was a big amount for a student then. I asked him what I should do with my money, because we were good friends. He told me not to do anything until he did a little research first.

Some weeks later, he came with a Globe and Mail (a Toronto newspaper) financial section and pointed to a penny stock (Quebec Sturgeon) and said, "Buy these shares! They found gold, but are not telling the public yet, because they are collecting back the shares from the market and very soon the shares will skyrocket!"

"How do you know this?" I asked cynically.

"I heard from the portier at the Communist party," he replied.

"C'mon, commie!" I protested, "How would the portier at the communist party know such things?"

"He talks to a lot of people and he knows a lot," Antti defended himself.

"I am not going to buy the shares the portier at the Communist Party has recommended!" I joked. And obviously, I didn't buy them.

Quebec Sturgeon shares jumped, after a few weeks, from 8 cents to 16 cents, the next day to 50 cents, the next day to one dollar and in a month's time, to exactly 16 dollars. Two hundred times the money! The Koran says: "Don't accuse God because he doesn't give you things. God gives you things and you must appreciate."

All the professors heard the story and one day, exactly six teaching staff came by my drawing table, stood in line and began rolling their thumbs.

"If you don't listen to the portier of the Communist Party, this is what happens!" one joked.

"Why didn't YOU buy the shares?" I questioned.

"Antti told only you. Not to us!" they joked further.

Anyway, if anyone bought the shares at eight cents, he would have two hundred times more money after a month. My thousand dollars would have become two hundred thousand dollars! This was a miracle indeed, but I had not wanted to risk my money and missed it. I should have bought at least for 200 dollars...40.000 dollars a month later would be a very big graduation present for me.

Chapter 14
No More Miracles in Canada

After my graduation, I moved back to Montreal. I worked for a year at architectural offices, including the design team for Montreal area postal plants. But I could not find a nice, permanent job, as architectural jobs were very scarce and always temporary.

I decided to take a vacation for a month or two to visit my brother in Brussels, Belgium, where he worked as the reception manager at the five-star Hotel Lendi. And later visit also Istanbul, where my mother and youngest brother and many relatives lived. I deposited my belongings at a friend's cellar in Montreal and moved out from my apartment. Upon my return to Canada, I would have no difficulty finding any apartment or room in Montreal, as it was a paradise for apartment seekers.

I flew to Paris and my brother and his fiancée came to meet me at Charles de Gaulle Airport. Paris is always fun. First, we had a dinner in Paris and then drove to Brussels. My brother and his fiancée were planning a trip to Istanbul as well to visit my mother and the rest of the family. We arranged the visas for the countries en route and started after ten days the long trip that should take us through Germany, Austria, Hungary, Romania and Bulgaria, to Istanbul.

Chapter 15
A Terrible Accident

We drove until Salzburg without problem. I had a strange feeling that in Salzburg a serious problem or incident would occur. My brother had a good friend there, who helped us check into a modest hotel and we decided to stay in Salzburg for a couple of days, before we continued to Vienna.

The night before our departure to Vienna, my brother and his friend drank a lot of beer in the hotel's bar and later my brother's friend insisted that we drive up to the mountain in Salzburg. It was already past midnight. Both he and my brother were quite drunk. The next day, we were scheduled to drive to Vienna at 9 am. I told my brother that it was too late to go for a drive, if we were to start for Vienna the next morning. And warned him and his friend not to drive in that condition. I had not drunk more than a few beers, but I have no driver's license, so I could not help them. I was worried that if they drove in the condition they were in, they may have an accident.

My brother said to me that if I want, I could stay in

the hotel and sleep, but they wanted to go to the top of the mountain in Salzburg. They drove off and I went to bed.

Early in the morning, the sad news came. My brother's friend had had an accident and he, my brother and his wife were in the hospital in Salzburg.

I took a taxi immediately to the hospital. My brother's friend was in very bad shape. Later, he had nine operations and could die. Thank God, he was saved. My brother's wife was also in bad shape. She also had several operations. My brother had managed to save himself, with only a few minor wounds, sitting behind the driver's seat. This is what happens when people drive when drunk.

We stayed for a few days more in Salzburg. My brother's wife and friend remained in the hospital and my brother decided to drive to Istanbul through Italy and take the ferry boat from there to Turkey. I did not join him. I had an open Eurailcard and started a train trip in Europe. God had spared me from the hell that they had lived through. I was very glad my brother had luckily survived the accident with a few minor wounds and a shock, naturally, but I was extremely sad his wife and his friend were severely injured and could have lost their lives. It was indeed a miracle for me that I did not go with them to this after-midnight ride. I had worked very hard to make them give up driving in drunken condition. They did not listen. If I knew that accident would happen, I would have called the police to stop them.

Chapter 16
The Swedish Miracle

My brother left Salzburg for Istanbul via Italy and I started my Eurail trip. I understood from my communications with him later, he had another minor accident while driving through Italy. The front glass of his car has blown off. I thanked God that I didn't accompany him.

My Eurail trip took me to many places in Europe. Coming to Stockholm from Berlin, I had a funny feeling in me. A voice said in me: "You'll find a job and stay in Sweden." I was coming to visit Sweden, see a close friend and his family whom I had known for many years in Istanbul. My friend was Turkish, his wife Swedish and they had two daughters. In Istanbul we were together nearly every day. Later, they came to Stockholm and resettled there. My actual plan was to travel around Europe, finish up my travels in Istanbul, stay for some time with my mother and brothers and then fly back to Canada.

In Stockholm, I called my friend and his wife gave me some very sad news: my friend had died. She welcomed me to stay with her for some days, which I did.

About a week later, time came for me to depart.

"Come to my office today for a pizza," my friend's wife said. "Let me invite you for a pizza lunch before you leave Sweden."

She worked for Samsonite and Luntmakargatan. First, I carried my luggage to the Central Station, deposited them in a box and then I went to meet her in her office. When I went to see her at twelve o'clock, she was busy. She asked me to come at one o'clock. "In the meantime, you can go to the next building, the employment office," she said.

I had no intention of looking for a job in Sweden. I had put my luggage in a deposit box and planned to take the night train to Hamburg to continue my travels.

"There is nothing else to see in the vicinity," she explained. "Maybe you meet an unemployed girl in the next building!"

"Oh, c'mon," I said. "I'm leaving tonight."

I left her, to meet again an hour later. Indeed, there was nothing to see around there. I entered the employment office. As soon as I came in, I saw two ads in Turkish, which said, "We are looking for Turkish teachers". I wondered why they were looking for Turkish teachers in Sweden. If they needed Turkish teachers in Germany, I would have understood, as there were many Turks in Germany. But in Sweden, I had not heard of any Turkish population. I noted down the phone numbers in the announcements and called them after the pizza lunch.

The one in Haninge Kommun invited me for an interview the same afternoon. I went. I was offered a job. The pay was good and they promised to help with the work permit, an extremely difficult thing to get at that time.

I brought my luggage back to my friend's wife's apartment. She was surprised. I asked if I could stay for a few weeks. She said it would be all right. The following days, I spent trying to apply for a work permit and the police gave me a temporary permit, as I had an international student card from Canada.

I started to teach immediately. After a three-month period, I applied for a regular work permit. Since I lived with my friend's wife, this co-habitation entitled me to a work and residence permit in Sweden. Before, I had no intention of staying in Sweden. There I was, settled in Stockholm with a job and a work permit and friends.

Next to the school where I was working as a Turkish teacher, for the children of the Turkish immigrants, they had built an experimental housing project. Although one had to go through a central registry in Stockholm, to find an apartment (the waiting time varied from five to fifty years or more), for that new housing project, there was a separate registry. One could apply locally there and get an apartment immediately. This was the only area in Sweden where one could get an apartment immediately. I chose a nice two room flat on the top floor, with a nice balcony. It was only one hundred meters from my job and one could be in Stockholm's downtown in half an hour, with frequent buses or suburban train. I sent some money to my friend in Montreal and he sent me my belongings. I stayed in that teaching job until retirement. I started an international business consultancy firm on the side, made big deals but got cheated. Then I started to write books. This book is my fourth.

My first book was titled, THE SECOND VENICE,

a humorous book published by Outskirts Press; my second book was titled, WISDOM IN SMILE, containing short stories, which is still waiting for further stories to be written before publication; my third book was a professional book titled, ARCHITECTURE AND EDUCATION: AN INTERFACE. I had also written quite a few poems, but only some of them being fine, they did not fill a book. Two of them were published in known poetry anthologies in the U.S.A.

I also wrote many articles: Some fifty articles in the biggest Turkish daily HURRIYET; a few articles on education in the Swedish teachers´ journal; a few international articles on peace and on intellectuals and social change.

I joined also a UN allied Non-Government Organization, I.A.E.W.P. (International Association of Educators for World Peace) and became its Associate Secretary General at international level and its delegate at the UN, Vienna and Geneva, for two years.

Later, I joined also The International Parliament for Safety and Peace, with Headquarters in Palermo, Italy, and became its senator and Minister Delegate.

All these engagements were on voluntary basis, with no pay.

I started also an international association named W.I.S.E. (World Intellectuals´ Social Establishment) with the aim to " protect the intellectuals´ rights and enhance their communications", which attracted many adherents from many countries, but did not survive due to lack of financing. Its manifesto was published in many countries though.

Chapter 17
Many Miracles in Sweden

As I have lived for thirty years in Sweden now, I experienced many small miracles here. I shall relate them one by one. Some of them happened in Sweden, some when I traveled to other places on my vacations – in Poland, Turkey, Switzerland, Finland, etc. They are interesting and manifold.

A Polish experience:

In the summer of 1976, I had met in Stockholm, a young Polish couple, both engineers. I helped them for a few days with board and lodging. They invited me to Warsaw. I already had good friends there and was planning to visit Warsaw. We altogether took the boat to Gdansk. Before that, they asked me for a small loan of sixty dollars and promised to pay me in Warsaw. I gave. When we arrived in Warsaw, they paid me only 3000 zlotys. The going rate on the street was 100 zlotys for a dollar. They said the bank pays normally 33 zlotys for a dollar in business transactions, 50 zlotys to the dollar if tourists exchange. I got cheated for

3000 zlotys. When I was returning to Stockholm, I overnighted in Gdansk, in its best hotel. I usually wake up early in the morning and take a promenade. I did the same in Gdansk. I went for a promenade at six o'clock. There was no one in the streets. A man was sweeping the foliage in front of the hotel. I noticed a small, colorful fold of papers among the leaves and the garbage. I took it. I opened it and saw it was one 2000 zloty and one 1000 zloty banknote. I was happy. 2000 zloty banknotes had not officially come out yet, but were being seen here and there and were being accepted, as they would become legal tender after a month or so.

Some two hundred meters later, an oldish pay-woman with a rose on her chest, was looking between her breasts for something. When I passed by, she asked me in Polish, something about 3000 zlotys. I told her in English, that I did not understand Polish. It was, I think, her pay, which she had put between her breasts and dropped by mistake in front of the hotel. It was the exact same amount that the engineer couple had cheated by me out of.

The next summer I went to Istanbul. I looked for some old friends' phone numbers in the telephone book, but did not find them. Two of them I had known in Toronto, one in Istanbul. One Sunday, I met one of them with his family at the restaurant of the Hilton. It was the first time I had lunch at the Hilton. He said it was the first time they had a lunch at the Hilton too. Had we both been regular customers of the Hilton Hotel, I would classify this incident as a coincidence. Under the circumstances, I classify it as a miracle.

During the same week, I met the other friend in the Delta Airline's office. And the third one I was looking for I met in a "dolmush" (the shared taxis which act as busses in Turkey). Someone tapped me on my shoulder from the back seat.

"Hello, Askin!" he said.

I turned back and saw Faruk Sipahi. It was an un-believable coincidence or a small miracle that I found all three friends within the same week.

A very interesting small miracle:

I think it was during New Year's Eve in 1978. I called a few dance halls to book a table, but everyplace seemed fully booked. Finally, I found a table at Alaadin, a popular dance hall of Stockholm.

"I'll keep the table for you until 9 pm," said the res-ervation man. "One minute past nine and I will give it to somebody else!"

"Ok," I said, "I'll be there by nine at the latest."

I dressed up, ate my dinner and while watching the news on TV, fell asleep.

The balcony door was open about 5-6 cm, no more. All of a sudden, a big explosion woke me up. A fire-cracker had entered into my living room through that small gap, right onto the floor and exploded there. I looked at the clock and there was only five minutes to the bus if I wanted to be at the dance hall before 9 pm. I hurried to the bus stop, wondering how a fire cracker would enter my apartment which was on the seventh floor, through a small gap in the balcony door and ex-plode to wake me up at the right time to enable me to catch the bus. When I reached the dance hall, the time was five minutes before nine. My table was waiting for me.

I sat and ordered a bottle of wine. The place was packed. Soon after, two ladies came to me and said,

"Are you alone?"

"Yes I am."

"Can we sit with you? There are no empty tables left. We would be happy to pay for your wine if you permitted us to share your table with us."

"I'd be happy to share my table with you," I said. "You don't have to pay my bill. But I hope you excuse me if I don't pay yours."

"No, no!" they said. "You don't have to pay for us at all. We are very glad to have found a place. We'll be happy to pay your bill."

"I pay my bill, you pay yours," I said. "If this is an acceptable condition, I'll be happy to have your company." We agreed. They sat. I danced with them. One of them said that if I would be kind enough to take a walk around the dance hall, perhaps other men would ask her for a dance. She said if men see we are sitting together, they wouldn't come and ask her. I laughed and accepted. I took a walk around the dance hall. They were both dancing with some men.

After a while they said the men they were dancing with were so drunk they hated them. Around midnight, as we had become good friends already, they asked me to accompany them to their apartment after the dance hall closes around 3 am.

"Oh, I won't stay that long," I said. "I must take the last train at 1 am."

They gave me their phone numbers and address and told me they will wait for my call soon, for a get-together.

I left the dance hall at half past twelve. To take a taxi to the suburb where I lived would not only be too expensive, it would also be impossible to find a taxi on New Years Eve.

I took the last train at 1 am and then a small bus connection to my neighborhood. I took the elevator to my floor, the seventh floor, I put in the key into the keyhole and all the lights went off. I understood the next day that there was a nationwide electricity breakdown, which lasted for four hours. I thanked God. What would have happened if I had gotten stuck when I was in the elevator or the train? God had helped me to reach the dance hall on time, and God certainly helped me to come home safely, just a few seconds before the electricity breakdown. It was impossible for me to regard these incidents on New Years Eve as coincidences. They were small miracles God had made.

Was it the same year or another year, I forgot, but a SAS plane had crashed at Stockholm Arlanda Airport, during takeoff on Christmas Eve. The plane was broken into three pieces and everyone came out alive. The next day, we read in the papers that the five year old daughter of the SAS pilot gave her father a ten crown banknote and congratulated him to be a good pilot. Incidents or rather miracles like that, prove there is a God and there is love. Those who think otherwise are wrong, because there cannot be millions, trillions, quadrillions, or an unlimited number of coincidences in the world, constituting the life, which we are experiencing.

Chapter 18
The Pillow

Living in Stockholm means also taking cruises to Finland often. Sometimes the cruise prices are really low. Boats are superb, large boats for up to 2000 to 3000 passengers, have nice cabins, many restaurants and pubs on board. I took such a cruise once – one of many – during my thirty years of residence in Stockholm. It was a 36 hour cruise to Helsinki, giving one twelve hours in Helsinki, daytime. One can do sightseeing, shopping, enjoy sometime in Helsinki's beach or restaurants or pubs.

Going to Helsinki, I met an architectural professor who worked for Nordplan in Stockholm and taught part time at the Helsinki Technical University. He had the other berth in the cabin I sailed in. This is how we met. We had a nice, professional discussion in the boat, being both architects. Coming back, he was still in the same boat, but in a different cabin. In my cabin there was another passenger.

I went to sleep in my cabin around eleven o'clock, took a shower and took the upper berth. About midnight came in a big sailor type drunk Finnish man, with tattoos on his arms and started to talk to me in Finnish first, and then when he saw I do not understand Finnish, in Swedish. My Swedish was very poor at that time. I answered him in English.

"I don't like foreigners at all," he said. "You damn foreigner! You also have black hair! I don't like black haired foreigners at all!"

The guy was drunk, was insulting me and I felt afraid.

"Well," I said. "As you don't like black haired foreigners, good night to you!" I pulled the blanket over my head and wanted to sleep.

He punched the mirror on the wall, shouted and swore and came near me and said, "I want to fight with you!"

"I don't want to fight, I want to sleep!" I replied.

He was insisting on bothering me. I felt really afraid. I thought of escaping from the cabin, but he had locked the door from the inside and was standing in front of it, with no intentions of letting me out. I thought my passport and money, which I had put in my pillow as I always do during such travels, would remain as a present to him, if I managed to leave the cabin. I did not have much chance to leave the cabin anyway, with him standing in front of the door, but in case I could manage to get out, I did not want to leave my passport and wallet behind. If I took out my passport and wallet from the pillow in front of him, he would see them and would probably take them from me. So I got up from the bed in my pajamas, took the pillow instead and sat my hand inside, holding my passport and wallet in it firmly. Suddenly a miracle happened. He stepped aside and the door was accessible now. I did not understand immediately why he stepped aside all of a sudden. Holding the pillow with my hand in, I approached the door, opened it and started to run toward the elevator. The sea was quite rough and the boat was rocking and pitching severely. I took the elevator to the top floor, where the captain's bridge is, and in the corridor leading to the bridge I saw an officer sitting in a room, counting the coins from the slot machines.

In my pajamas, my hand in the pillow, I entered his room and started to tell him what had happened. He was also very astonished to hear what had happened. While telling him the story, I realized why that drunken man had stepped aside and let me out. Because he had thought probably I had a gun or a knife in the pillow and did not want to risk his life. Otherwise, he was determined not to let me out and fight with me.

"Wait awhile, let me finish counting the coins," the ship's officer said. Then I'll help you."

It took him about a quarter of an hour to count the remainder of the coins. Then he called the ship's police or the security officer. We went all together to the cabin. I took my belongings and I was given a luxury cabin in one of the upper decks.

"I want to sue this man," I explained to the ship's officer and the security officer.

"As you see," they said, "the sea is quite rough now. We'll help you in the morning to get this man's identity and do what is necessary. I slept in my new cabin.

In the morning I met the architecture professor in the breakfast lounge and it was more interesting to discuss with him than running after that drunken man and the ship's security officer. I thought, while going out from the boat to land, I could talk to the police and try to catch that drunk man and do the necessary thing. I was next to the exit in the boat, when the boat was docking. That drunken man also stood in front of me, and was ready to get out of the boat as the first man. When the boat docked, we both got out. He, hurrying to go through the customs and the police, and I, was doing my best not to miss him. When we both were passing in front of the passport police, I changed my mind for the following reasons and gave up the idea of reporting him: One, I had no witness to the case. He could say I was not telling the truth and deny what he did. Two, when one officially reports someone to the police, he has to give his name, address and identity number on the report, a copy of which is always given to the other side. This is a major point of complaint in Sweden among the public and many fear to give his name, address and identity to the other side. For this reason, many do not report criminal incidents to the police. This is against the human rights, actually, and I don't understand why this is so in Sweden. So, I let the man go.

Chapter 19
Money! Money! Money!

As "every beauty has its fault" according to a Turkish proverb, I have mine too. Unfortunately, I gambled too much in my life. In thirty years I lost about 300,000 Swedish crowns, or some 40,000 US dollars. I am a non-smoker. If I had smoked a package of cigarettes per day, it would have cost me more. Of course, if one does not smoke, it does not mean one has to gamble. I could have saved this money and lived a more comfortable life in my retirement – if my books do not get published. (Or even if they got published, as promoting the books cost so much!) I could have bought a nice car, but I am not so enthusiastic about driving. In Stockholm, public transportation is quite satisfactory. I could have traveled, of course, with that money, although all my life was spent traveling. I used twelve Eurail cards in Europe, most of them for a month, a few for two months; I used thirteen Interrail cards for a month, and I think I have some fifty separate train tickets from my travels to Paris or Malaga or Barcelona or Roma or Istanbul or London, and scores of plane tickets within Europe and to and from North America. I still could travel. Now, there is no need to worry over the spilt milk and I should try not to spill any more milk, I think.

However, I played in nearly every casino in Europe, from Travemunde to Lindau or Bonn or Berlin; from Monte Carlo to San Remo and Nice; from Scheveningen to Stockholm or Istanbul. Sometimes I lost; sometimes I won. Of course, mostly I lost, like everyone else.

Once I lost one thousand dollars in Monte Carlo. But in San Remo I recovered half of it and in Nice, the other half. Just before I went into the Nice casino, I heard a voice: "Go in and play big." I went in and put some money on 28 and won. Then I won again on 31 and left.

In Berlin I had lost 500 dm once. The next day something pulled me again to the casino. I had only fifty marks left in my pocket, before I returned to Stockholm. I put some of it on 21 and won, and again I won on 18 and left the casino with 500 dm, which I had lost the day before. All these could be coincidences. But look at this and decide for yourself if this was a coincidence or a small miracle:

I was at the Stockholm Sheraton Hotel, one evening, as I went there often to have a glass of wine and listen to the piano music. I got hungry, but I did not have the money to eat there. I had some fifty crowns left, and one would need at least 250 to have a simple dinner.

I went to the roulette table, bought 50 one crown chips. At that time one dollar was equivalent to five crowns. In Sweden, until the new casinos opened, one could only play with one-crown chips. Later they raised it to 2.5 crown chips and then to five. Now in the newly opened casinos, one can play for large sums. I placed ten crowns on and around a single number. I won. Then I placed ten crowns again on and around a single number and won again. I continued in this way and won exactly nine times on single numbers. After nine winnings I had lots of money. Before I left the table, the following things happened:

1) After I won for the fifth time in a row, everyone who was playing at that table left playing and receded and bowed to me. I asked them, "Why are you doing this?"
"We know what we are doing!" they replied.

2) A man gave me his chips and asked me to place them for him. I did. He lost.

3) The casino manager came. He asked, "Is it you who won nine times on single numbers?"
"Yes," I said, with a lot of chips in my hand.
"I have been in this business for forty years," he said, "and I have never seen anyone win nine times on single numbers."

Then I went to the Sheraton's restaurant, ordered a nice dinner and a bottle of wine and enjoyed it. There was still money left. I played with it and lost.

I know the Koran and the Bible forbid gambling and I know it is not right to gamble. I admit my mistake and I minimized my gambling to ten dollars a week… I hope God forgives me. I thank God for having helped me win sometimes to cover my losses and give me sometimes the money I needed. Here are some more gambling stories.

Once I had a lunch in a Chinese restaurant in my neighborhood. I do not carry cash usually and pay with credit cards, so that I do not play the slot machines. After the lunch, I thought of how nice it would be if I had one hundred crowns to play the slot machines. All of a sudden I noticed something under the bar, about ten meters away that could be trash or a banknote. I stood up and went to the bar and exchanged a few words with the restaurant's owner and picked up what I saw. It was a one hundred crown banknote! I went and played the slot machines and lost of course, as one mostly loses if one plays the slot machines, since they are there to make money for their owners.

And once, after I played the slot machines and lost all my money, I thought how stupid I was, as I had not even kept fifty crowns for a pizza. Right after that, going out of the pub I found a fifty-crown banknote. I found money many times on the streets just when I needed it. As much as I can remember, a 100 crown banknote three times, 50 crowns once, several times 20 crowns, once 60 crowns in Stockholm and in Toronto twice 10 dollar bills and once 2 dollar bill… Once in Geneva, Switzerland on Christmas Day I found 70 Swiss francs when I sent my Christmas cards at the station's post office, which paid for an extra day in Geneva and I could finish up my business talks that day.

Once, during a night bus travel from Montreal to Boston, I woke up to go to the washroom in the rear of the bus. Everyone was sleeping in the bus except one passenger toward the middle of the bus. I was sitting in the front. Something came under my foot as I walked and I picked it up. It was a thick wallet full of banknotes. I could not think straight, as I had just awakened. It was probably a wallet that had fallen from a passenger also sitting in one of the front seats. The man who was sitting in the middle of the bus said that it was his wallet and took it. Later, I regretted that I gave it to him, as it was most probably not his, and most probably belonged to one of the passengers sitting in the front where I had found the wallet. There was a sign above the driver "Strictly Forbidden to talk with the Driver". Everyone was sleeping. I decided to ask the passengers when we arrived in Boston. I slept like everyone else. When we did arrive in Boston, I awoke and people had already started to leave the bus. I had no chance to find out who was the owner of the wallet. After many years, I am still regretting that I gave the wallet, most probably to the wrong person. This was his "small miracle". It is impossible to think straight when one wakes up after midnight to go to the toilet in the bus. Normally, if I could think clearly, I would of course check the wallet for an ID and control it with that other man´s name etc. before handing it out to him.

Once I sent one hundred crowns to the Red Cross by postgirot in Stockholm. It was the last money I had left. I was going to get my salary the next day anyway, I thought. After I sent the postgirot envelope, I remembered that I had no bread at home. If I had remembered it a few minutes before, I would not have sent one hundred crowns to the Red Cross, but buy bread. Right at that moment, I saw a one hundred crown banknote in front of me while I was coming out of the post office. I picked it up.

Once, I needed vacation money. Within a one-week interval, I won one thousand crowns twice in Sweden's Penninglotteriet.

Sometime during my first ten years in Sweden, I

won one hundred crowns nine times in the subsequent lottery drawings of the bank, which drew as the winners, the birthdays of the clients. Every month, one out of three hundred and sixty five days of the year had a chance to bring one hundred crowns to the clients born on that day. My birthday came nine times in a row.

Chapter 20
The Lotto Prize

We had a conflict with my mother that lasted a few years. She had made me angry with her injustice, economically, and for her preference to take the side of my younger brother over me and my other younger brother. Friends and relatives had criticized her for this. As I expected her to behave perfectly in such situations, and as she had disappointed me, I had decided not to talk with her. This silence lasted for several years. She had no intention to apologize and she did not seem to care whether or not I talked to her. This silence, though, seemed logical to me (even a respected doctor friend had understood and approved of my behavior) brought pains to me and I suffered for a long time, even though it was she who was guilty! I understood later, that she too had not lived an easy life after this conflict and reverted often to tranquillizers. I don't understand why people make mistakes and suffer and cause others to suffer for their mistakes and never apologize.

But, after three years of not talking to her, I saw no way out of this conflict. She would not apologize. Then one day I thought perhaps I should break the silence by creating another small conflict with her. This way we would talk again and at least I would give her a chance to apologize. If she still did not, well I could still prolong my silence to her, but if she did apologize then we could be friends again.

I called her up one evening and told her (within measure) bad words and accused her of being a bad mother for being unjust to her sons and not thinking of them and for not calling me to apologize. She defended herself that she was my mother and she did not need to apologize. I told her that that was wrong; that a mother or son must apologize to the other, whoever makes a mistake. I told her that I needed her help and sometimes I missed her, but I did not feel like talking to her because she made a very big mistake toward me and did not apologize.

I do not remember if she apologized after that or not, but at least I had broken the silence at last and had spoken to her after three years!

The following week I won a little over 60,000 Swedish crowns from the lotto, about 7500 dollars, which was very important to me. I called her and asked her to meet me and help me draw the money from the bank. She came and we met and I got the sum from the local bank. She asked me, "What are you going to do with all that money?" I sensed that she was insinuating that I should give her some sum., but she had more money than I had and did not really need any handouts from my side. Anyway, I gave her fifty dollars to be nice. I do not know if she cursed me for that or not, but I lost all that money, even a little more, gambling in the coming years. If I knew I would lose that money gambling, I would have given half to her and half to the Red Cross or another relief organization of some kind. Maybe I will next time.

Chapter 21
A Small Miracle on
Jesus Christ's Ascension Day

Year: 2000. Day: June the first. I was dreaming that I was showing the Holy Koran to a group of five or six young people from the ex-communist countries.

"This is the Holy Koran," I said to them. They listened with interest, but showed me another copy of the Koran, published in a communist country.

"This is the Koran published in our countries," they said. I looked at it. It had a big, half page painting on the lower right page. It looked like the art of old Renaissance painters, with half naked women lying around.

"No," I protested, "This is not the Koran at all. The Koran has no pictures."

"It is not so bad," they insisted. "Look, if you look at the pictures from this angle they disappear. If you look only from this angle one can see them."

"This is absolutely impossible," I said. "The Koran has no pictures."

At this point, I was awakened by the roaring sound of thunder. "Oh my God," I said as I woke up, "it must really be raining hard!" It was a little after three a.m. I went to the window and saw nothing but a clear sky!

One is usually drowsy right after one is awakened. But that time, my head felt perfectly clear. I was even astonished how clear my head was right after waking up! I was astonished at the roaring thunder-like sound from the sky, which lasted about ten minutes. It could not have been a plane's engine, as the sound of a plane's engine is much less compared with what I was hearing. In this quiet Swedish suburb there was neither a single soul on the street, nor a passing car. The roaring thunder-like sound came from a perfectly clear sky with no clouds and lasted about ten minutes.

It was God's voice, I thought, waking me up from my dream where a lie was being told about the Koran.

Chapter 22
Help From Mormon Angels

A drunken landsman had threatened me once in the neighborhood where I lived in Stockholm. I replied quite hard to him and this angered him and he continued threatening me wherever and whenever he saw me. I took the matter up to the police. Finally I put a friend in between, who knew this drunk, threatening man and he told him this: "Askin is asking if he should sue you or will that warning be enough for you to stop threatening him?" That put a stop to his threats, but I had become rather depressed because of his repetitive threats.

At that time I lived alone. I prayed to God to introduce me to a nice, lively girl who would cheer me up.

After some days, on my way from the station to my home, I was stopped by two beautiful Mormon missionary girls. Their American accent was so apparent in their Swedish, we immediately switched to English. Soon after, we agreed to meet in my apartment a few days later.

I prepared some lunch and we had quite a nice discussion about religions. They were happy to give me information about Mormons and I was happy to receive the Book of Mormon, which I read together with the Bible and the Koran. They again joined a party I gave to some members of the Canadian Club in Stockholm, and everyone was happy to meet them. So my prayer was answered, as these beautiful Mormon missionary girls, who studied at the University of Utah at Salt Lake City, really cheered me up. Their names were Sister Johnson and Sister Kelly. If this book gets published, I'll try to find their addresses and send them a copy.

Chapter 23
A Real Business Miracle

I n my trip to Istanbul in the summer of 1987, I visited my nephew very often. He had a nice café in Besiktas, frequented by the high brows of the locality. They sat and played cards or other games, chatted, drank tea, read newspapers. It was a nice neighborhood café, which attracted many businessmen also.

One day, talking to a businessman there I found an opportunity to tell him what I was trying to do with my company in Stockholm, in my free time left after teaching. Hearing from me that I had good contacts and high expectations of pulling off a big deal (I had sold three airplanes to an airline and was denied my commission; I had entered into business transactions with a wealthy Arab sheikh which had not paid any profits yet; and I was cheated in a cement deal from Russia) he asked me if I can find a connection with a shipyard which could build four ro-ro vessels, as Turkish Cargo Lines was looking for such new building vessels and had just advertised. My job would be to locate a proper shipyard, obtain their representation for Turkey; his job would be to follow the business in Turkey, obtain the necessary information, ensure the offer properly reaches the Turkish Cargo Lines and we would split the commission. This seemed like an impossible dream.

First of all, I could not imagine any reputable shipyard that was not already represented in Turkey. Secondly, all the shipyards (most were lying idle at that time) would read the Turkish Cargo Line's announcement in the Lloyd's Journal and would apply themselves to build such vessels. They would not need me. The businessman told me all this was true, but he had done such ship sales business before and gave me his card. He said, "If you happen to find an interested shipyard, give my card and tell them you have a good connection in Turkey to follow this business and maybe they will be interested to pursue this business through us."

Upon returning to Stockholm, I had completely forgotten about this business, but I had kept this businessman's card in my wallet.

One Sunday afternoon, I was sitting in the lounge of the Sheraton Hotel in Stockholm together with my good friend Alfred who was a lecturer in Arabic language, at the Stockholm University. We had met at the Stockholm International Club and become good friends. He is the author of the Arabic-Swedish dictionary (unfortunately, he is now deceased.) I was telling him about my trip to Istanbul and have also mentioned about this shipbuilding business. "I guess I have to forget about this deal," I commented, as all shipyards have representatives in Turkey.

The lounge of the Sheraton was practically empty. Other than us, a gentleman was sitting at the next table.

After awhile, this gentleman approached us and

asked if we had a match to light his cigarette. Alfred lit his cigarette (Alfred did not smoke, but always carried matches to light the cigarettes of ladies, etc.) The gentleman continued, "Excuse me. I happened to hear what you were talking about. I am sorry to interrupt you, but I did some business previously with a German shipyard. This is a small, but an old and very well recognized shipyard. I know its owner. If you wish, I can call him and tell about your business and ask if he would be interested. It will take about ten minutes. If you'll be here for another ten minutes, I will call him up now and can tell you the result."

Alfred and I looked at each other. It came as a very big surprise. I told the gentleman he would be welcome to call his friend, the owner of the German shipyard and we would wait for him. He went to call his friend and came back after ten minutes.

"The name of the shipyard is Neue Flensburger Schiffbau Gesellschaft," he said. "And the name of its owner-general manager is Mr. H.R. He is very interested to hear about the new building deal you talked about. He will be here in Stockholm tomorrow afternoon at this address. This is their Swedish representative's address. If you like, you can meet him tomorrow at five pm at this address in Stockholm and discuss this business. If you happen to make any business with this shipyard, please think of my commission too." He gave me his name and address in Malmo. He said he was busy at the moment with some construction job in East Africa, but his Malmo address was his permanent base, where he was reachable anytime.

I went to the address he gave me in Stockholm the very next day at 5 pm. Mr. H. R. was there and we sat and discussed the new building vessel business for the

Turkish Cargo Lines. Mr. R. said that his company had a representative in Turkey, but that he heard of this business first through me and he would be interested in appointing me as a temporary, additional representative for Turkey for two years. A nominal commission would be given to me, which I would share with the Turkish businessman who had talked about this business with me. He ordered a secretary to write an agreement and he signed and gave it to me,

I could hardly believe it. Suddenly I had become the representative of a German shipyard for two years! I called that Turkish businessman and told him I had found a shipyard willing to enter the international bid the Turkish Cargo Lines has announced.

"Good," he said, "You see, you manage it."

In a few months, the German shipyard prepared the necessary drawings and an offer to the Turkish Cargo Lines, which we presented to them, to participate in their international bid. What happened then? Well you do not have to wait for the result for months, as we had to do, you can hear about it here and now. Among some hundred and fifty or sixty offers, seven were selected, after a technical and financial scrutinizing of the offers. We were among these seven. Then, Turkish Cargo Lines gave the project to build the vessels to a Polish shipyard. Their price and conditions of cooperation must have seemed attractive. But, right after the international bid was over, there was a big reaction and a series of protests in the Turkish press, as Turkey had bought vessels from this shipyard previously and they were not satisfactory technically, the press articles said. Shortly after, the decision to buy the vessels from the Polish was annulled and the Turkish Cargo Lines made a new decision to buy to ro-ro vessels from a Norwegian shipyard at a price of US $86 million each. Our price, the price of the Neue Flensburger shipyard was DM 65.5 million. The price difference was huge. Were the Norwegian vessels so much superior to the German vessels to substantiate such a huge price difference? As I am not a shipping specialist, I don't know. But, I don't think so.

Chapter 24
A Pleasant Small Miracle

Once, I was on my way from Germany to Stockholm, by train and I had a few hours in Lubeck, between two trains. I went to the town square and sat in a fine garden pub. A while later came an angel-like beauty to take my order. I have never seen an angel, but after seeing this waitress, I thought I had seen one! I ordered a beer, I prayed to God to whisper to me her name so I could surprise her when she came back. Some strange voice told me her name was I.S. (not fair to mention it here). When she brought my beer and I paid her, I asked her if her name was I.S. She became very surprised. She asked me how I know that. She said she had just started to work there that evening, a few hours ago, and not even her colleagues in the pub knew her name. She became very curious from where I learned her name.

I said, "If you really want to know, sit with me for a few minutes and I shall tell you." She did. I said that I had prayed to God to whisper me her name and God did! She did not believe me. She took a nametag from her breast pocket, which also confirmed her name.

"I don't even put my name tag on," she said. "People learn my name and try to contact me. I have a boyfriend I am living with. Please tell me from where you found out my name! Because I never met you before, and as you said, you are transit passenger traveling to Stockholm and it is the first time you have been in Lubeck," she said. She became very curious. I insisted that it was a small miracle of God. She explained that she was studying at the Conservatorium in Kiel and her boyfriend also was a student in the same conservatorium. I invited her to Stockholm.

"Maybe someday I will come," she said, "but I shall come with my boyfriend."

I sat for a couple of hours in that pub. When the train time approached I left the pub with tears and she was still very, very curious as to how I knew her name. That incident was proof to me that God is capable of everything.

Chapter 25
Miracles of Finland

Once, when I was traveling from Vienna to Warsaw by train, I met a nice, young intellectual Finnish woman who was teaching Finnish at Warsaw University. We became friends.

Many years later, I was visiting Helsinki with one of the thirty-six hour cruises from Stockholm. I had taken the boat at six pm on Saturday from Stockholm, which brought me Helsinki Sunday morning. I had eight hours at my disposal in Helsinki. I was scheduled to return to Stockholm with the same boat in the evening. These are quite modestly priced, pleasant cruises. One can enjoy the good food in their many restaurants, take a drink in their pubs, dance in their disco and meet many people. In the summer, they offer a fantastic view of the Stockholm archipelago and an opportunity to sunbathe on their decks. These are huge boats for about two or three thousand passengers and their cabins are quite comfortable too. On Sunday the Helsinki streets were all empty. When walking on its main street, Mannerheimintie, whom did I see? My good

89

friend, Riita K., who taught Finnish in Warsaw. It was a very big surprise for both of us.

"What are you doing here in Helsinki, Askin?" she screamed when she saw me. There were only two of us on the street.

"I came with a cruise," I explained. "I'll go back in the evening. What are you doing here on a Sunday, when all the Helsinki streets seem to be empty?"

"I am going to a summer cottage with an architect girl friend," she went on. "I am here just for a few minutes to fetch something. Then I'll go to the bus terminal and take a bus to the summer cottage we rented. My friend will also come to the cottage later today. It is a pity you are going back tonight, otherwise you would be welcome to the cottage with us."

"Are you sure?" I asked. "Maybe I can cancel my return tonight. There are plenty of boats every day to Stockholm and I can take a boat back tomorrow, maybe."

"We'd be very pleased," she said cordially. "We'll stay there for a week. You can stay with us as long as you like."

I had only a small bag with me containing the necessities for the cruise. But they would be sufficient for a few days more during a cottage vacation by a lake near Tampere. I accepted the invitation with much gratitude. Two hours later we were on a bus with Riita K. heading for their summer cottage near Tampere.

We arrived, after a rather shaky bus ride, at their rented cottage. There were a few cottages by a lake and we greeted the other inhabitants first, before we settled in the cottage that Riita and her friend had rented. A few hours later, Riita's friend arrived. Another Riita! Riita H. was an architect working in one of the most reputable architectural offices in Helsinki. Being of the same profession, we started a hearty discussion with her.

Riita K., the linguist, was a very nice, humorous girl with extreme capacity for theater. She could imitate nearly anyone. I never forgot how she imitated how different nationalities walked.

Riita H. was a young, proficient architect. She told me of her trip the previous year on a yacht, where there were some ten or twelve men (all her friends) and only one woman: her!

We had a very nice time together, preparing nice dinners together, discussing until the late hours everything and anything.

One day, they prepared the sauna and invited me to it as well. I had been in sauna once before in Canada, in Sudbury, Ontario, when I visited an architect there. It was a tough experience for me. Although I slept very well for twelve hours after it, and when I woke up I felt reborn. I did not want to go through the same experience again, as it could be too tough for my heart. It is good to sweat and throw out all the poisons in the body and relax and sleep very soundly thereafter, but from extreme heat into the cold waters of the lake, and back to the heat sounded for me a little risky. So I did not go into the sauna.

A day later, they asked me if I wanted to do anything special there. I replied that I always wanted to bicycle around the Finnish lakes. "It is easy to arrange!" Riita K. said. "But we only have two bikes. You have to choose one of us and then you can realize your dream and bicycle around the Finnish lakes for a day or two!"

It wasn't easy to choose one of them, as they were

both very nice. I didn't want to leave one of them behind either, as it would not be polite. But they insisted. They obliged me to choose one of them to bicycle around the lakes for a day or two.

After a few hours, we were on our way to a two-day bicycle ride around the Finnish lakes. We packed some sandwiches, took some water, our bathing suits, and some money, as we would have to overnight it in a youth hostel on the way and eat in the cafeteria. About an hour later, when climbing a steep road, I felt extremely tired and breathless.

"Come on, Askin!" Riita H. encouraged me. "We have two days of bicycling in front of us and you got tired after one hour. There I was! In the beginning of realizing my dream of bicycling around the Finnish lakes with a nice Finnish girl and I had gotten tired already after an hour of bicycling.

"Are there many such steep roads on the way?" I asked, breathing with difficulty.

"Most of the way is like this!" Riita H. explained. "The whole way is up and down. I always hated roads with zigzags. This was the first time I had experienced roads up and down, in Finland.

"There is no way I can continue," I complained. "Maybe we get off the bikes and carry them to the top of the road and ride them again coming down," I said.

"Come on, Askin!" Riita H. protested. We can't always carry the bikes each time we hit a steep hill! Try hard!" she encouraged. I was a little ashamed. I could hardly pedal longer. I prayed to God to make a miracle so this terrible bike ride would come to an end. About five minutes later it started to rain. What a rain! Riita H. this time herself said, "We can't continue in this rain!"

I was so thankful to God for this great miracle. "Let's return to the cottage!" Ritta H. said. We had seen a run-down mill a while before. We took refuge in it.

"What a film!" I remarked. "Only the music is missing!"

The rain provided its own music, especially falling into the mill through the holes in the mill's roof. We waited there for a couple of hours. Then, when the rain stopped, we headed back to the cottage. An hour later we were back at the cottage.

"What happened?" Riita K. asked.

"Askin couldn't continue after an hour!" Riita K. answered.

"It was you!" I protested. "It was you who said 'Let's go back' after it started raining!"

Chapter 26
Marmaris Bus Incident

Marmaris is a small, charming resort town in southwestern Turkey. Once, I visited it for ten days. I have a good entrepreneur friend there, whom I know from Montreal, Canada and the town itself is quite appealing with its gorgeous beach, nice climate, landscape and the tourist crowd from every corner of the world.

After ten days, I booked a seat on a night bus to Ankara where I was going to meet a minister friend. They usually smoked in buses in Turkey then, and I thought a night bus could be comfortable from this point of view, as the passengers would sleep during the night and would not smoke. Exactly the opposite happened.

When I boarded the bus, it was full of forty passengers. Someone said they were construction workers returning from a job. As the bus started, each and every one of them started smoking. The windows of the bus were all sealed, impossible to open and then I was among forty heavy smokers who had no intention of sleeping.

It was past midnight. As the bus rolled on, forty passengers lit one cigarette after another and the bus was filled with a thick white smoke. Now, I understand, it is forbidden to smoke on the buses Turkey, like in other civilized countries, but then, it was free to smoke or if there was a regulation against smoking it was not being followed.

I did not know what to do. I talked to the driver's assistant and he regretted that there was nothing to do. I felt so badly, as I was choked from the smoke. I could die if the situation went on. There were no stops en route, where I could get off the bus and go back to Marmaris and try another route, like traveling by bus to Izmir first and then from there to Ankara. And on the buses to and from Izmir the situation could be better. When I had traveled from Izmir to Marmaris, one could open the windows of the bus and despite the day traveling, not so many smoked in the bus. From Izmir to Ankara, one could take the train also, which usually had non-smoking compartments, or one could fly.

I started to pray to God and ask him to make a miracle to save me from this situation. I said, "God! If you don't want me to die, you have to make a miracle now!"

All of a sudden, the smell of burning rubber was noticed in the bus. The driver's assistant got up from his seat in the back, to check what was burning. I alerted him as well. "Something is burning. You'd better check it," I said.

"I know," he said. "I'll ask the driver to stop so we can check it."

The driver stopped the bus. All the passengers went out. It was like a blessing to breathe the fresh air again.

The time was about 1 am.

"It is the rubber band of the cooler, in front of the motor," the driver's assistant said. "It's burned."

"What are you going to do now?" I asked. "You must certainly have a spare one."

"No," he replied. "We don't have a spare one. We'll order one, with the driver of one of the buses going to Marmaris and our office there would surely send us a new rubber band with the first bus from Marmaris."

"How long will that take?"

"Well, at least four hours, if we are lucky!"

"I have to be in Ankara tomorrow morning," I explained. "My minister friend is waiting for me."

"We'll find a way out for you," the driver's assistant replied.

He suggested that we stop the next bus passing from there towards Ankara, and I get on it, if there is a seat. That could also mean a few hours waiting and also there would be the same risk with all the passengers smoking.

"In that case, I recommend you to make a compromise," the driver's assistant suggested. "You take one of the minibuses passing here, to Denizli, a town near there, and go to a hotel and take the morning train to Ankara from Aydin."

"All right," I said. After half an hour, we stopped a minibus passing from there, I got on it, and after a half an hour's ride we were in Denizli. I checked into a hotel and took the train to Ankara the next morning. I was one day late to my appointment with the minister friend. But at least I was saved from the thick, white cigarette smoke cloud in the bus, which, for sure, would have killed me if I had continued on that bus.

Chapter 27
Three Typewriters

I was working as a teacher of Turkish language in Stockholm for the children of Turkish immigrants. I had an English keyboard typewriter, which my friend in Montreal had sent me with my other belongings, but I could not use it to prepare lessons or the exams for my students, as the Turkish language has six distinct letters that do not exist in the English alphabet. I had written an article for the Swedish Teachers' Journal "Lärartidningen" talking about my methods of teaching, problems, etc. A publishing company's editor had read this article and made me an offer. He said he could supply me with a Turkish keyboard typewriter if I wrote some article for their journal "Hemspråk och Svenska" ("Mother tongue and Swedish"). At that time the Swedish government was very generous with subsidies to such publications. I thanked him and accepted the manual FACIT typewriter with the Turkish keyboard. This was indeed a miracle that enabled me to work efficiently as a teacher.

Then I acquired a Casio CW-25 electronic typewriter to use for my business correspondence and literary writings in English. After some ten years, this typewriter broke down. At that time, I had started to write this book, "The Small Miracles".

I looked around all the shops to buy a new Casio CW-25. Its typing was excellent and its price was OK. Unfortunately, the manufacturing of this typewriter had been stopped and it was impossible to buy one. It was impossible to have the broken one repaired, either.

There I was, without a typewriter and with a lot of business letters to be written, and most importantly my book, "The Small Miracles". I could not find another sort of quiet typewriter either. (So that the neighbors would not complain, as sound isolation was very poor in the apartment where I lived.) One day, I was going to visit a psychiatrist friend. I knew he also had a Casio CW-25 typewriter. A wish passed through my mind, that my psychiatrist friend would somehow buy a new typewriter and would sell me his old Casio CW-25. That was perhaps a crazy wish, but I was going to the psychiatrist anyway, wasn't I?

In his office, I noticed a new, big typewriter. "What happened to your old Casio typewriter?" I asked enthusiastically.

"It is impossible to find ribbons for it," he explained. So I bought this one."
I told him the Casio CW-25 would type on fax paper without a ribbon, or he could use special heat sensitive paper that would not necessitate the using of a ribbon.

"Ah, well, I bought this new one now," he said.

"Would you sell your Casio CW-25 to me?" I explained that mine was broken.

"Oh, well then. You can have mine for free," he said.

There I was, experiencing a second typewriter miracle. I promised myself to include a chapter for that in my book, "*Small Miracles*".

When I progressed with my writing the book, that typewriter, too, broke down. Then I had met a new friend, Gudmund, in a political party where I had become a member. He lent me his Smith-Corona. It ensured me to complete my book and it even ensured, with its loud sound, my neighbors, that I was writing my book.

In this age of computers, I am still using typewriters, because I don't like to deal with the different components of the computers of which I understand nothing. My neighbors objecting to my heavy typing which is heard in this sixty year old prefabricated apartment house, where I suffer living and in my ignorance and poverty which forbid me to buy a computer, will probably end up my writing career, I thought. My last chance would be to write by hand and ask a secretary to type it.

Just when I was in a critical situation and definitely needed a computer – which I did not know how to use, I found on the table in the café a brochure of DELL. It said, great year-end discounts were being made. At the same time, I met a young Turkish engineer who promised me that he would help me to set up the computer and show me its basics, if I bought one. That would mean a significant saving for me, as the computer company would charge a great deal if they set up the computer in my home.

I bought the computer and a printer. Yusuf, my young Turkish engineer friend set it up and showed me basics of how to write and how to deal with the internet and send and receive e-mail. Luckily enough, the same month when I subscribed to the internet, they too, had a special offer – no entrance fee and one month free of charge use of internet!

All this was unbelievable for me. I had bought the computer and the printer at a really low price, an engineer friend whom I had just met that week had set it up free of charge for me, and the internet subscription had offered a special price the same week!

Well, with all these coincidences or small miracles, whatever you would prefer to call these, I had no alternative but write books.

Chapter 28
A Small Miracle in Istanbul

The last time I visited Istanbul, I went to the same small hotel where I always stay: AS HOTEL, right in the middle of Beyoglu, Istanbul's main shopping street. Its owner is a religious person and I wanted to talk with him about the Islam religion during my stay, now that I had gotten interested in the God's religions. As he goes to a nearby mosque often and meets many Moslems, I wanted to ask him how the average Moslems thought about God's other religions. I know that Moslems are very tolerant and respectful to the Jews and the Christians, as the Koran advises, "Not to differentiate among God's prophets and God's books", but I wanted to have his opinions and impressions on that. We were quite good friends, as I had stayed in his hotel many times. I had thought how nice it would be if I had both the Bible and the Koran, where I could show him many similar paragraphs in both of these Books, which brought the God's message to mankind: Peace, love, justice, respect to the parents, to the governments, to the self, to others and to the environment;

acceptance of a single God and praying to God, for his benevolence, mercy and small miracles. Fasting, sacrifices, sharing with others what God has given to one; being truthful, abstaining from adultery and theft; loving one's neighbor as one loves himself; believing in life after death, self control and tolerance and modesty-all seemed to be the same central values in all the religions of God. A few differences or deviations did not seem at all to be any reason for wars and conflicts among God's religions, nor within the same religion.

I arrived at the hotel and checked in. The proprietor greeted me and we started an enthusiastic chat about the new happenings in Turkey and about our lives.

"What are you doing these days?" he enquired.

I told him I had started a movement to unite the religions of God, under the name The Believers, to promote a nation of Abraham, where all the believers of God would unite. That seemed to be a good way towards peace.

He said this idea is not new, but certainly is a good idea to work with. The Ottomans always respected and regarded the Moslems, the Christians and the Jews as equals. As a matter of fact, in Istanbul (Ortakoy) there is a mosque, a church and a synagogue adjacent to each other, on the same block.

"I want Christians also to read the Koran, and the Moslems to also read the Bible," I said "In this way, seeing that their books are the same, and came from the same God, they will stop fighting with one another."

He took a small Bible from his bookshelf. "I, for one, am reading both the Koran and the Bible," he said.

"Really?" I enquired. It was a Bible in Turkish. "Where did you get this?"

"Someone must have dropped it in front of the hotel," he said. "About half an hour before you came, I found it on the street."

"Interesting," I murmured.

Half an hour later, a street salesman came, selling Korans. I looked at them and he was selling the edition of the Koran, which I had missed buying in 1960, and later it was sold out. There it was, brought to me by a street salesman.

"This was out of print," I said. "When was it published again?"

"Recently," he said, "and it became very popular." I bought it. Now I had a Bible and a Koran, permitting me to talk to my friend, the proprietor of the hotel the whole evening, about our new movement, The Believers.

I think this was a small miracle. Don´t you?

Chapter 29
My Birth was a Miracle

I cannot conclude my book without mentioning my birth, as this book would have been impossible to write without me.

When my mother was pregnant with me, doctors have told her something was wrong with me and they must cut me into pieces and take me out or else she would die. My father had accepted that, as he preferred to have my mother continue living, but my mother had rejected this proposal of the doctors and preferred to give birth to me, in spite of this serious endangerment to her life. Doctors had told her that she would die for sure, if she gave birth to me.

Finally, they met a midwife, who advised them, based on her many years of experience, that there was nothing wrong with my mother's pregnancy, and that she would have a perfect birth! Obviously my parents have trusted her with my birth rather that going to the doctors at the hospital and my mother has given a perfect birth to a son – that's me! In Stockholm, an enquette has been made among women who gave birth to a child at Södersjukhuset, one of Stockholm's hospitals, and the rate of satisfaction among women who trusted a midwife seemed higher than those who trusted a gynecologist. Hence, "this hospital used midwives for childbirth to a good extent", a newspaper article had said and of course in case of complications, gynecologists were consulted.

So, I had come to this world, with some sort of a miracle. My mother says all births are miracles, which is true.

The cycle of life, in its every phase, is a miracle.

Chapter 30
Copper Colored Energy Bulk

Once, as I was about to go to sleep, I felt a very special warmth in me and I felt loved – for five, ten seconds. Then, a coil of energy, in copper color, left me and said, "I shall come again."

I don't know if that was my imagination or an act of God. This was a mystery for me. Then, some months later, I read a paragraph in the Koran which was describing this experience and that "everyone will experience this."

While writing this chapter I looked again for this paragraph, but could not find it. It can take a very long time to find a paragraph in the Koran. I am envious of those imams and priests and rabbis who know their books by heart and can immediately point to the relevant paragraphs when necessary. If I find this paragraph before this book reaches a publisher, I shall write its number, or else the reader can ask an imam, or perhaps find this paragraph number in one of the future newsletters of The Believers, or while reading the Koran.

Chapter 31
More About "The Believers"

The following pages are the manifesto of The Believers.

If you believe this movement is interesting to you, you can communicate with us at the following address and we can further our thoughts and a possible cooperation thereafter.

> *The Believers*
> *E-mail address:*
> abrahamsnation@yahoo.se

The Believers' Manifesto

We believe in God and in all the God's prophets and books that we have on hand. The psalms which came to prophets David, the Old Testament which came to prophet Moses, the New Testament, which came with prophet Jesus, and the Koran, which came through the prophet Mohammed. We also believe in the Book of Mormon, which came through the prophet Smith. It is possible Buddha and Confucius were also prophets and the books of Buddhism can also be the acts of God, as their contents are so similar to the Bible and the Koran. By Nirvana, they mean God. We also believe in sciences and the arts, which are the products of human intelligence. The culmination of God's words and the sciences and the arts should lead mankind on his path of life toward the future.

Love, peace, cooperation, sharing with other what God has given to one, respect, self control, humility, justice, protection of the body and soul and the environment; wisdom, knowledge, truth; belief in miracles of God, praying for God's mercy and benevolence, creating beauty, are the key elements of all God's religions. Thus, they are also the key principles of The Believers. Life, death, growth, movement, energy, time are the basis of existence. Change is its proponent. We do not distinguish among God's prophets. We read God's books with interest and conviction that they show us the right way in life. We bear in mind the Koran is the last direct message from God to people and there are no serious controversies among the books of God as God is one. They are here to generate a culture with the same good values of ethics. Not to generate wars, disagreements or conflicts. No matter what, we thank God for what God has given us. And we are united under one God. We pray to God for mercy, benevolence, help, and to make for us small miracles and guide and protect us on our path of life.

All the religions of God have been misunderstood by its followers to a good extent, as well as by the followers of the other religions of God. The reasons are: politics, traditions, changes in the elapse of time, economic profiteering of the nations, groups, powerful individuals; misunderstandings due to translations, interpretations, ignorance or lack of proper research, etc. There is plenty of room in all the religions of God for research, to correctly understand God's religions. This is one area of interest for The Believers.

The second area of interest is to unite all the believers of God. Many ask, "Why should I leave my religion and join The Believers?" Our answer is that you should not leave your religion, but bring it with you to The Believers. Enrich us, The Believers, with your religion, as we believe in all the religions of God! We do not look at Moslems, Christians, Jews and the Zerdusht (believers in the prophet David and the psalms) or the Mormons, or the Buddhists as enemies of one another. The Bible says, "all those who believe in God, from their hearts, are brethren!" The Koran says, "All those who believe in God are brethren." Enmity, disagreements, conflicts, seeing one's own religion as superior to the other religions, are in the minds of those who misunderstand their own religion and the other religions of God! Not in the books of God! The Believers is a call to all the believers of God, no matter which one of God's religions they belong to, to unite! Study of all the books sent by God will simply encourage this and erase all misunderstandings among the religions. Aren't there differences among the religions? Yes. Some minor differences... Mostly the differences are due to the elapse of time, misunderstandings, misinterpretations, lack of research and are minor in nature, as God, who orders peace and love and brotherhood in all his books, cannot have meant wars, enmity, conflicts and hatred!

The third area of interest for The Believers is to bring a possibility of social contacts to its members, to save them from isolation, loneliness and by enhancing their communications with one another, to inspire and enable them to grow and realize their functions of existence! This is to take place both locally (regionally), and globally. If there are other intelligent civilizations in the universe, The Believers is interested to carry its ambitions universally.

Eventually, The Believers can grow also as a political party and as an ethical organization for planning; and can manifest itself in the areas of sciences and the arts and designs. The Believers is the assurance of self-realization, a healthy existence, in recognition of God, sciences and the arts and the designs.

The Koran: "One who knows science understands this book better."

Prophet Mohammed: "If it is necessary to go to China to find and learn the science, go there!"

The Koran: "The place for those who create beauty is the paradise."

The Bible: "No one will come to me in darkness!"

The Koran: "All the religions of God, on Earth, have equal value. The religion in the other world is Islam." Islam means the religion of those who believe in peace and God. Christians, Moslems, Jews, Zerdusht, Mormons, Buddhists – all who believe in God – are Moslems, as Moslem means "a person who believes in peace"

In the Koran, Jesus says to his twelve apostles during the last supper, "Thank God we are Moslems." Sora: 5 (Maide) Paragraph III.

The Koran, Sora 2 (Bakara), paragraphs 3, 4, 5: "Those who believe in the other world, pray properly, and abstain from those which we have given as material benefits, and share them with others, and those who believe in what we have sent to you (The Koran) and also in those books we have sent previously, and believe in God and the other world definitely, are on a path of salvation of God and have reached happiness."

We invite all interested to communicate with us, enrich us with their beliefs and cooperation and helps. May God help us, The Believers, to follow God's orders, which are clear in all the books sent by God.

May God help us find peace and love and truth and justice and cooperation and help us progress in our sciences and add onto our arts, which will carry us with their beauty to the paradise.

May God forgive us for our sins and mistakes, give us strength in following the path of God, and cherish us with small miracles, to help us in the difficulties we experience. Amen.

THE BELIEVERS

CPSIA information can be obtained
at www.ICGtesting.com
Printed in the USA
LVHW03s0010250918
591277LV00001B/6/P

9 781598 001006